Beautiful Feet

Beautiful Feet

The Story of
Maud Elizabeth Hoyle

*To my dearest and long-time friend, Judy —
Be blessed and be a blessing!
Love,
Michele*

6/18/18

Michele Cash Russo

Beautiful Feet: The Story of Maud Elizabeth Hoyle
© 2018 by Michele Cash Russo

ISBN: 9781980560029

CREDITS

Scripture quotations marked (ISV) are taken from the Holy Bible: International Standard Version®. Copyright © 1996-forever by The ISV Foundation. All Rights Reserved internationally. Used by permission.

Scripture quotations marked (KJV) are taken from the King James Version of the Bible.

Scripture quotations marked (NIV) are taken from the Holy Bible, New International Version®, NIV®. Copyright © 1973, 1978, 1984, 2011 by Biblica, Inc.™ Used by permission of Zondervan. All rights reserved worldwide. www.zondervan.com. The "NIV" and "New International Version" are trademarks registered in the United States Patent and Trademark Office by Biblica, Inc.™

Scripture quotations marked (NLT) are taken from the Holy Bible, New Living Translation, copyright ©1996, 2004, 2015 by Tyndale House Foundation. Used by permission of Tyndale House Publishers, Inc., Carol Stream, Illinois 60188. All rights reserved.

Cover design: Elizabeth Loring Design and Creative Services
Interior design: Stephen Sigety
Set in Bookman Old Style and Bell MT.

This book is dedicated to my great-grandmother

Ida Virginia Hoyle

who consecrated her infant daughter Maud to God,
taught her about God's love, grace, and mercy,
and encouraged her as she took each step in her journey
as a devoted disciple of Christ.

Contents

List of Photographs/Illustrations	vi
Acknowledgements	ix
Preface	xv

Part One: Maud's life

Chapter One: First Steps	3
Chapter Two: A Firm Foundation	13
Chapter Three: Preparing for the Road Ahead	21
Chapter Four: Plant My Feet on Higher Ground	30
Chapter Five: Another Step Forward	41
Chapter Six: Go!	46
Chapter Seven: How Beautiful Are the Feet	66
Chapter Eight: Finishing the Race	95
Epilogue	111

Part Two: Maud's Writings

Thesis: Practical Christianity	117
Sermons	
Salvation	145
Two Gardens	155
The Love of Christ to His People	165
The Lord is Looking	176
History of the Columbus Avenue Church	181

Appendices

Appendix A:	
Abbreviated Hoyle Family Genealogy Chart	188
Appendix B:	
Boxwell-Patterson Examination, April 19, 1902	189
End Notes	195
Bibliography	205

List of Photographs and Illustrations

1. Maud Elizabeth Hoyle	xiv
2. Stained Glass Window in Columbus Avenue Church	xv
3. Full window at Columbus Avenue Church	xvi
4. Maud's Handwritten Vita	2
5. House where Maud was born	3
6. The Hoyle Children	4
7. Alpha Schoolhouse No. 13	5
8. Springfield City Market	7
9. Keys to Hoyle Stall at City Market	7
10. Hoyle home on Columbus Avenue, Springfield, Ohio	8
11. Benson School House	8
12. The Hoyle Family, circa 1900	10
13. Boxwell Graduates, 1892–1902	11
14. I Am His Ring	13
15. Philip Otterbein	16
16. Martin Boehm	16
17. Jacob Albright	17
18. Women in 1909 Bonebrake Seminary Graduating Class	26
19. Maud's Graduation Photo, 1909	28
20. Surveyor's Description of lot	31
21. Groundbreaking of the Columbus Avenue UB Church	33
22. Columbus Avenue United Brethren Church, circa 1912	34
23. Page from Sermon, "Two Gardens"	37
24. Sermon Outline	38
25. From the Springfield News-Sun, December 27, 2009	39
26. Springfield City Hospital, circa 1910	42
27. Maud, circa 1920	44
28. Map of the African continent 2011	49
29. Street in Freetown, Sierra Leone, circa 1921	52
30. Village in Sierra Leone, circa 1921	53
31. Cloth weaving in Sierra Leone	54
32. Schoolhouse in Rotifunk	57
33. Maud's Passport and Travel Papers	61
34. Ship leaving New York harbor	63
35. Wharf at Liverpool	65

36. Locals carrying trunks on head	67
37. Map of Rotifunk Mission Farm	68
38. Martyrs Memorial Church, Rotifunk, Sierra Leone	69
39. Rotifunk Mission Compound	70
40. Diagram of the mission house	71
41. Women washing clothes in river	72
42. Dispensary in Rotifunk	73
43. Hatfield-Archer Dispensary, Rotifunk, Sierra Leone	74
44. Yanco(?) Betty Smart, Ellen	77
45. Maud Hoyle holding Maude Smart (pastor's baby)	77
46. Maude Smart and Nora Caulker	78
47. Maude Smart feeding baby leopard	78
48. Map of Sierra Leone	80
49. Sewing class in Moyamba	81
50. Dress Dorothy Hoyle wore to see Maud off, 1924	85
51. Passport, issued March 28, 1927	88
52. Hospital in Jiama	89
53. School boys in Jiama	89
54. Article by Maud Hoyle	92
55. Article about Maud Hoyle	93
56. Maud and her mother Ida	95
57. Masonic home and Rickly Memorial Hospital	97
58. Friendship Quilt	99, 100
59. Maud outside Rickly Hospital, Ohio Masonic Home	101
60. Marble Hall, Otterbein Home, circa 1910	102
61. Main lounge, Medical Building, Otterbein Home	102
62. Typical Room, Otterbein Home, circa 1960	103
63. Missionaries at the Otterbein Home, 1951	103
64. Nurses at the Otterbein Home, 1957	104
65. Maud outside Columbus Avenue Church, circa 1950	105
66. Maud's Death Certificate	107
67. Maud's marker, Newcomer Cemetery	108

Acknowledgements

The journey that I have taken in researching and writing this book has been long but truly filled with joy. Much of the joy has come from the many people who have helped me along the way.

First, I must thank my mother, Dorothy Hoyle Cash, for sharing stories of my great-aunt, Maud Hoyle, and for keeping many of Aunt Maud's personal effects, including her Bible, some of her writings, and many photos. I also thank my mother for the meticulous genealogical research that she conducted on the Hoyle family. I have incorporated her work about Aunt Maud's early life into this book. I only wish that she were still alive so that I could thank her in person.

Having spent most of my adult life as a librarian, I have often spoken about the importance of libraries and archives. As a user of these treasure troves in the last few years, I am even more convinced of their value. I am deeply indebted to a number of institutions and the librarians, archivists, and historians who preserve and manage the collections. The first place I visited was the United Theological Seminary Library which also houses the Evangelical United Brethren Heritage Center. Harry Burchell found information about Aunt Maud's time in seminary, as well as providing me with *The Evangel* which had several articles written by or about Aunt Maud when she was in Africa. Harry also suggested that I go to the Ohio United Methodist Archives. There the archivist, Carol Hollinger, helped me find information about Aunt Maud's official ministerial status over the years. Carol also alerted me to Jeremy H. Smith's book, *The Staircase of a Patron: Sierra Leone and the United Brethren in Christ*. Smith based much of his book on the diaries of Lloyd Mignerey who served as a missionary in Sierra Leone at the same time Aunt Maud was there. I was able to read Mignerey's diaries and letters at the

Otterbein University Archives where Stephen Grinch assisted me. Mignerey's writings were invaluable to me and I was especially thrilled when we found his drawing of the mission house which pointed out "Miss Hoyle's room."

Others who helped me with my research are Linda Frazer from the Brighton United Methodist Church which has preserved the records of the Columbus Avenue church; Frances Lyons-Bristol, archivist at the General Commission on Archives and History at Drew University; Marge Henn, archivist at the Otterbein Home Heritage Center; and the great librarians and staff at my home library, the Franklin D. Schurz Library at Indiana University South Bend. A special note of thanks to Maureen Kennedy who was always able to get me the Interlibrary Loan material I needed, no matter how obscure.

I appreciate my cousins, John Hoyle and Susan Hoyle Lizza, for sharing their remembrances of Aunt Maud with me. I thank my niece, Faith Schiffer, for transcribing Aunt Maud's sermons and other writings which appear in Part Two of this book. Great-nephew Austin Smith compiled the "News of the Times" which helps put Aunt Maud's life in some context of what was happening in the world at the time.

A very special thanks to my sister, Sheila Skimmerhorn, who helped with the research. She also, along with my dear friends, Susan Antonovitz and Janet Fore, read and commented on my drafts and offered encouragement throughout the process. I also am deeply indebted to Stephen Sigety for his expertise in creating the interior design of this book and to Elizabeth Loring of Design and Creative Services for her beautiful cover design.

One of the very special blessings that I experienced as I conducted research for this book was finding and connecting with Rosalee May Karefa-Smart. She is the grand-daughter of Pastor James Alfred Karefa Smart, the local minister who served with Aunt Maud in Sierra Leone. Our connection grew even closer when we discovered that we share the same birthday. I am immensely grateful that she reviewed my chapters about Sierra Leone and gently suggested more sensitive terminology to describe the indigenous people and groups in Sierra Leone. Thank you, my anam cara.

Last, and most certainly not least, I am grateful for my husband, John Russo. He supports me in countless ways and makes my life worthwhile every day. There is no one else I would rather have by my side as we travel on this journey of life. I could not have completed this book without his support.

I heard the voice of the Lord, saying,
Whom shall I send, and who will go for us?
Then said I, Here am I; send me.
—Isaiah 6:8 (KJV)

I thank Christ Jesus our Lord,
who has given me strength,
that he considered me trustworthy,
appointing me to his service.
—1 Timothy 1:12 (NIV)

1. Maud Elizabeth Hoyle

Preface

July 15, 1958. It was a small country church, but it was filled to overflowing with persons there to pay their respects. The casket in the front of the altar held the body of a petite, white-haired woman, Maud Elizabeth Hoyle, who was my great aunt. She had been highly revered in the family. My sisters, cousins, and I all knew that we needed to be on our best behavior around her. Not that she demanded it—but because we knew that she was a special lady and we were taught to hold her in high regard.

The funeral was held in the Columbus Avenue Evangelical United Brethren Church in Springfield, Ohio. While I don't recall the words that were spoken that day, I do remember looking at one of the stained-glass windows in the church that had her name[a] on it—proof to this not quite yet eight-year-old that Aunt Maud was also revered by others outside of our family. This was really no surprise. After all, she graduated from seminary in 1909 and became an ordained minister. She was responsible for seeing that this very church was built, and she was its first minister. Later, after studying to become a nurse, she went to Sierra Leone as a missionary. That stained-glass window was just a small token of how esteemed Aunt Maud was in this community.

2. Stained Glass Window in Columbus Avenue Church. Photo by Sheila Skimmerhorn.

Of course, all that happened long before I was born. By the time I was in the picture, she had become a res-

---

[a] The stained-glass window contained a misspelling of Aunt Maud's name by adding an *e* at the end. This inaccuracy was repeated many times throughout her life in both formal and informal documents.

ident of the Otterbein Home. This was (and still is) a retirement/nursing home in Lebanon, Ohio. I remember visiting her in her small one-room apartment. She was quite short, no more than five feet tall, and she had beautiful snow-white hair. At times, she would be in her nurse's uniform—white dress, white hosiery, white shoes—on her small feet, and her white nurse's cap sitting atop her white hair. She wore very thick glasses and always had the sweetest smile on her face. I also remember that we would take her out to eat at the Golden Lamb (the oldest inn in Ohio, which continues to serve fabulous meals today). It was always a special day when we traveled to see her.

While I never knew Aunt Maud when she was most active, I heard stories about her for years, even after her death. However, it wasn't until I grew older that I really began to understand what a trailblazer she was, and I wanted to know more about her. I knew the family lore and I wanted to verify

3. Full window at Columbus Avenue Church.

and record as many of those stories as possible. I also wanted to try to learn more about her life. Why did she get educated beyond the 8th grade when her older brothers didn't? What was her life like as a seminary student and as a minister? Did she ever feel discriminated against because she was a woman? How had she developed a faith so deep that she was willing, as a single woman, to spend ten years in Africa? Was she ever afraid? And what did she do there (besides helping to deliver 200 babies)? These were just some of the questions I had when I started this project. While I couldn't find answers to all, my research led me to far more information about Aunt Maud than I ever imagined existed. I am excited to share what I've learned with my family, a few of whom also remember Aunt Maud. The narrative that follows weaves the new material into the stories that our family has always heard about this amazing woman—a woman who walked hand in hand with God throughout her life.

Michele Cash Russo
December 18, 2017

Part One:
Maud's Life

Maud Elizabeth Hoyle

Father - Stephen A. Hoyle - Born Nov. 25, 1855. Died Dec. 11, 1919.
Mother - Ida V. Dowden Hoyle - Born Feb 12-1857. Died July 27-1936.
Brothers { Wilbur S. Hoyle - Born Aug 11-1880 - Died Feb 2-1958.
{ Walter J. Hoyle - Born Aug 11-1880 - Died Sept 20-1953.
Maud E. Hoyle Born Dec. 15-1881 —
Charlotte R. Hoyle Born April 24-1886 - Died Feb 27-1904.

Maud E. Hoyle born Dec. 15-1881 at Springboro, Ohio. Spent 12 yrs. at Trebein, Ohio. Attended Graded School and Reformed Church of Alpha while there. Moved with the family to Springfield, Ohio in 1893. Finished graded school with Boxwell examination June 12-1897.

Converted April 27-1899 through the J.A.H. Circle and joined the Lagonda U.B. Church. — Transfered to Columbus Ave U.B Church in 1912.
Life Patron of Women's missionary Soc. March 17-1928
Graduated - International S.S. Association March 31-1905.
Bonebrake Theological Sem. 1906 - Graduated May 8-1909
Quarterly Conference License - June 11, 1908
(Rev. C. A. Kurtz)

Annual Conference License Aug. 27, 1909 Bishop Belle
Ordained - Aug 26, 1909 - Dayton, Ohio. 1st Church.
Pastor of Columbus Ave. U.B Church - 1912 - 1917.
Springfield City Hospital Training 1917 Graduated May 20, 1920
Missionary - Sierra Leone, W. Africa - 1921 - 1931.
Attended mother who became blind - 1931 - 1936.
Nursed at Masonic Home Springfield 1936 - 1940
Nursed 2 ladies in Dayton - 1941 - 1944
Nursed at Otterbein Home Jan 1, 1945 - Dec 31, 1956
Retired Jan 1-1957 - Relieved when needed since.
Became member of Otterbein Home Feb 20, 1952.

4. Maud's handwritten vita.

Chapter One:
First Steps

*Train up a child in the way he should go;
even when he is old he will not depart from it.*
— Proverbs 22:6 (KJV)

Maud's story begins with her parents, Stephen Ursheline Hoyle and Ida Virginia Dowden Hoyle.[b] They both grew up in Frederick, Maryland, where Stephen was a merchant and worked in the store owned by his future father-in-law, Zachariah Dowden. After Stephen and Ida were married in 1879, they followed some of their siblings to Springboro, Ohio which is about sixteen miles south of Dayton. While it's uncertain what Stephen did for a living there, he probably worked as a farmer, although he owned no property.

It was in Springboro where Stephen and Ida began their family, first with twin boys, Wilbur and Walter,

5. The house where Maud was born.

---

[b] Much of the information in this section about Maud's early life was taken from the genealogical research conducted and compiled in 1992 by Dorothy Virginia Hoyle Cash, Maud's niece.

6. The Hoyle children.

born on August 11, 1880, and then their first daughter, Maud Elizabeth, born on December 18, 1881. While still an infant, Maud became seriously ill. When there was little hope for her survival, her mother knelt beside her and prayed, promising to dedicate Maud to God if God would restore her to health. Maud did survive, and Ida never forgot her promise. She taught Maud about God and set her on the path to become a devoted follower of Christ for all her life.[1]

The following year, the family moved about twenty-five miles north to Trebein, Ohio which today is part of Beavercreek Township, just east of Dayton. While primarily a farming community, the town supported three flour mills, one distillery, and various saw-mills.[2] Stephen worked as a miller at one of the grist mills. Four years later, their second daughter, Charlotte (known as Lottie) was born. The family stayed in Trebein for twelve years.

The Hoyle children went to Alpha School No. 13, built in 1883 at the corner of Memorial Drive and Alpha-Bellbrook Road. The twins probably started school in 1886. This was a typical one-room school house where the essentials of reading, writing, and arithmetic were emphasized. Maud's niece, Dorothy Hoyle Cash (Walter's daughter), recalled hearing the story that Walter and Wilbur, never seeing their teacher go to the "little house out back," decided that their teacher was "just too nice to have those needs!"

7. Alpha Schoolhouse No. 13.
Photo by Verlon Dale Cash

During this time, the family began attending the German Reformed Church in nearby Alpha. It is uncertain why they went to this church since Ida had been reared in the Presbyterian Church and Stephen in the Catholic Church. What is certain is that both wanted their children to develop a strong Christian faith.

The German Reformed Church had emerged from the Protestant Reformation and was part of the Calvinistic family of churches. The German Reformed Church eventually merged with other similar traditions to form the United Church of Christ. (An interesting note is that William Otterbein, the founder of the United Brethren Church, had been a German Reformed pastor at one time.) The Reformed Church in Alpha that the Hoyles attended is now the Beavercreek United Church of Christ and its current building is located on Dayton-Xenia Road in Beavercreek.

On October 13, 1893 (when Maud was twelve), her father purchased five acres of land on Columbus Avenue on the east side of Springfield, Ohio, and this is where Stephen and Ida settled for the rest of their lives. The land was rich and black, and Stephen became a truck farmer. The entire family helped with the farming and Maud often recalled how she loved to walk barefoot in the dark, moist soil. She also told how she memorized the books of the Bible while she was planting potatoes. The family also raised chickens. Ida would dress the chickens and make corn mush and hominy and take these along with their onions, potatoes, rhubarb, and other produce to sell at the year-around indoor City Market in Stall No.76. Great-Great-Granddaughter Faith Schiffer now has the keys to their booth.

One of the crops that the family grew was white celery, which is sometimes referred to as "blanched celery."[3] This was (and still is) considered to be a delicacy and the Hoyles had a reputation of growing the best in the Springfield area. White celery seems to be a primar-

8. Springfield City Market

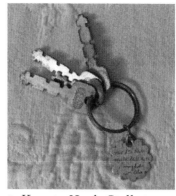

9. Keys to Hoyle Stall at City Market
Photos by Faith Schiffer.

ily English vegetable, although it isn't as popular there as it once was. It is grown by digging a trench and gradually banking up the dirt against the shoots, protecting the stalks from sunlight, thus making it white. White celery is generally considered to be much more difficult to grow than the green variety, but the results are thought to be superior, being delicate and tender with a nutty taste and hints of artichoke. Because it is harvested in the winter, it was common to serve white celery in a vase at Christmas dinner during Victorian times.

The family lived in a house near the farm which is still standing today. Maud's niece, Dorothy Hoyle Cash, remembers the house having a kerosene stove, a

10. Hoyle home on Columbus Avenue, Springfield, Ohio

melodeon organ (a small portable, reed organ that preceded the American pump organ[4]), a pie safe (often with vinegar pie—a custard pie flavored with apple cider vinegar), and lots of books. Over the years, these books often became Christmas presents for the grandchildren. Ida was more educated than Stephen and she could recite poetry by the hour. Maud credited her mother for instilling a love of learning and poetry in her.

The Hoyle children finished their schooling at Benson

11. Benson School House

School located at the intersection of Tuttle Road and Old Columbus Avenue. They had to walk almost four miles each way to get there. Records show that A. B. Graham, founder of the 4-H Club, taught at this school in the early 1900s, but he probably was not there when Maud attended. This was a typical one-room schoolhouse which offered classes from grades 1–8. School attendance was not mandatory until 1921 and most students, including Walter and Wilber, did not go beyond the eighth grade before then.

When Maud was sixteen, she studied for and passed the "Boxwell Examination" on June 12, 1897. The Boxwell-Patterson Examination was Ohio's first proficiency exam.[5] Under a law passed by the Ohio General Assembly in 1892, students in rural Ohio who passed the Boxwell exam after completing the eighth grade could attend any high school in the county without paying tuition. This exam, which took an entire day to complete, tested students in spelling, language, reading, writing, arithmetic, geography, physical geography, grammar, United States history, and physiology. Although a copy of the 1897 exam could not be found, the one given in 1902 was located.[6] The entire 1902 exam is in the Appendix for those interested, but for now, here is a sampling of the questions:

> —Why did the southern states claim the right to secede from the Union? Which states seceded? Name five important battles of the Civil War.
> —What difficulties were experienced under "The Articles of Confederation"?
> —Name all the bones of the shoulder and arm.
> —Trace the blood from the right hand to the left hand.
> —I gave my agent $162.50 with which to buy corn at 62 ½ cents a bushel, after deducting his commission of 4 percent. How many bushels did he buy?
> —How much will it cost to carpet a room 21 feet by 14 feet, with Brussels carpet 27 inches wide, at $1.20 per yard, the carpet to be laid lengthwise of the room, 3 inches being lost in matching each strip?

—Name the mountain ranges running from Spain eastward through southern Europe and Asia.
—What crops are being harvested at this season of the year in Australia?

Statewide, only about 30% of the students who took the exam passed in any given year. At Benson School, only four students in ten years passed and Maud and her sister, Lottie, were two of them (see the chart to the right). It seems that both Maud and Lottie were not only bright, but also that they benefitted greatly from their mother's emphasis on reading and education.

In the early Twentieth Century, teachers in some school districts in Ohio were required either to have graduated from high school or to have passed the Boxwell Exam. This suggests that for some, passing the Boxwell exam was equivalent to a high school diploma. As there is no indication that Maud attended high school, this must have been the case for her. Her early education prepared her well for the next steps she would be taking.

12. The Hoyle Family, circa 1900: Wilbur, Ida, Maud (standing), Stephen, (young child, unknown), Lottie, Walter.

Boxwell Graduates from Springfield Township's Schools

No.	Name of School	1892	1893	1894	1895	1896	1897	1898	1899	1900	1901	1902	Totals
1	Pleasant Ridge	1	1	1	1	0	2	1	0	0	1	0	8
2	Reids	0	0	1	1	4	0	0	1	1	0	3	11
3	Sinking Creek	0	0	0	2	0	0	8	2	0	1	0	13
4	Congress	0	1	2	2	1	0	0	0	0	2	0	8
5	Cross Roads	0	0	0	0	0	0	1	0	0	1	0	2
6	Benson's	0	0	0	0	0	1	1	1	1	0	0	4
7	Possum	0	5	0	1	0	5	1	2	0	3	2	19
8	Mill Creek	0	0	1	0	0	0	0	1	0	0	0	2
9	Rockway	2	0	0	0	2	0	6	1	2	5	7	25
10	Snow Hill	0	0	0	0	0	2	0	1	0	2	0	5
11	Victory Grove				1	0	2	0	0	0	0	1	4
12	Locust Grove						0	1	1	0	2		4
	Eleven Years Total	3	7	5	8	7	12	18	9	6	15	15	105

Pleasant Ridge.— Nellie Mechlin ('92), Frank Skillings ('93), Madge McDonald ('94), Byron Skillings ('95), Mary Laybourn ('97), Nellie Blanche Moore ('98), Lillie McDonald ('97), Geo. Moore ('01).

Reids.— Minnie Schuster ('94), Loui Schuster ('95), Grace Schuster ('96), Naomi Smith ('96), Mary Tuttle ('96), Chas. Schuster ('96), Edward Newton ('98), John O'Neal ('00), Edith Newton ('02), Alice Kramer ('02), Flora Tonkinson ('02).

Sinking Creek.— Nellie Yeazell ('95), Mabel Otstot ('95), Offie Valentine ('98), Laura Valentine ('98), Park Kunkle ('98), Maud Trout ('98), Nora Kunkle ('98), Burns Heffner ('98), Ellen Sultzbaugh ('98), Carrie Runyan ('98), Will Yeazell ('99), Grace Heffner ('99), Daisy Trout ('01).

Congress.— Maggie Hinkle ('93), Edith Crabill ('94), Jane Collins ('94), Maud Musselman ('95), Frank Knaub ('95), Olin Ronken ('96), Asadora Braden ('01), Glenna Crabill ('01).

Cross Roads.— Mary Kerns ('98), Henry Middleton ('01).

Benson's.— Maud Hoyle ('97), May Hause ('98), Grace Thomas ('99), Lottie Hoyle ('00).

Possum.— Lottie Moore ('93), Harry Otstot ('93), Lida Moore ('93), Albert LeFevre ('93), Sidney Griffith ('93), Ida Griffith ('95), Arthur Kissell ('97), Maud Haley ('97), Kate Griffith ('97), Frank Burkhead ('97), Clifford Haley ('97), Dola Gram ('98), Albert Walters ('99), Jas. C. LeFevre ('99), Vira Paige ('01), Alice Gray ('01), Ada Riebert ('01), Burt Gram ('02), Anna Burkhead ('02).

Mill Creek.— Walter Minnich ('94), Edward Walters ('99).

Rockway.— Jessie Holcomb ('92), Biddie Sheehan ('92), Herman Eberhart

13. Boxwell Graduates, 1892–1902. Provided by the Clark County (Ohio) Historical Society.

News of the Times

1881 – Chester Allan Arthur begins his term as President following the assassination of President Garfield on September 19.
1881 – Billy the Kid is killed in a western standoff after murdering twenty-one men.
1881 – Edison Illuminating Co. brings light to New York City for the first time.
1883 – Pedestrians step onto the Brooklyn Bridge for the first time.
1886 – Statue of Liberty is dedicated.
1886 – Coca-Cola goes on sale for the first time.
1888 – The Washington Monument is completed in Washington, D. C.
1888 – Benjamin Harrison is elected President.
1889 – Eiffel Tower opens.
1890 – Idaho and Wyoming admitted to the Union.
1892 – Grover Cleveland, who had served as President from 1885–1889 is re-elected.
1895 – The X-ray is discovered making it possible to photograph inner organs and bones.
1896 – William McKinley elected President.
1897 – The cause of malaria is determined to be a parasite carried by the Anopheles mosquito.

A few of the active artists, musicians, and writers at this time: van Gogh, Cassatt, Rodin, Tchaikovsky, Sousa, Kipling, Mark Twain, Robert Louis Stevenson.

Chapter Two:
A Firm Foundation

> *Teach me to do your will, for you are my God.*
> *May your gracious Spirit lead me forward on a firm footing.*
> — Psalm 143:10 (NLT)

Sometime after Stephen and Ida moved to Springfield, the family began attending the Lagonda United Brethren Church located on Mitchell Boulevard. Again, it is not known why they chose this denomination, but it quite likely was because it was the closest church to their home. It is also possible that they were familiar with this denomination, as it was founded in their hometown of Frederick, Maryland.

Maud joined the I.A.H. (I Am His) Circle at the church. This international organization was founded by David C. Cook, a Chicago publisher of Sunday School literature. He began the I.A.H. Circle in order to help young people learn how to live faithfully for Jesus throughout the week, and not just on Sunday mornings. It was important to Cook that the Gospel message appeal to one's intellect as well as to one's emotions and the materials that he published for the I.A.H. Circles reflected this. He also created a ring designed to help the young people always to remember to apply what they had learned at church.[7]

14. I Am His Ring

It was through Maud's involvement with the I.A.H. Circle that she truly understood the depth of God's love for her and for the entire world. She was eighteen when she took the single most important step of her life—one that would indeed eventually take her on "a journey of a thousand miles." On April 27, 1899, Maud converted, accepting Christ as her Savior. At that time, she completely devoted her life to Christ, vowing to go wherever she was led. It was also through the I.A.H. Circle that she began to feel the call to become a missionary. How grateful Ida must have been, knowing that while she had dedicated Maud to the Lord years before, now Maud had taken this step for herself.

Little is known about Maud's life between her conversion and her entering into seminary in 1906. She undoubtedly continued to live at home and helped her parents. Her brothers, Wilbur and Walter, worked at the McCormick Reaper plant (now known as Navistar International) and then later at the McGregor Greenhouse. In 1902, Walter married Lida Garrety and a year later, Wilbur married Henrietta Fissel.

Tragedy struck the family when Lottie, Maud's younger sister, died of tuberculous on February 27, 1904, at the age of 17. John Hoyle (Wilbur's grandson) recalls that his father, Paul, told him that Ida and Stephen had taken in a border who coughed a lot. Speculation is that he had tuberculosis and that Lottie had contracted it from him. Lottie, like her sister, was a highly esteemed and devoted member of the Young People's Society of Christian Endeavor. This Society wrote a resolution noting Lottie's "high morality and lofty ideas" and resolving to imitate her "many excellent virtues and her increasing love and devotion to the church and Christian Endeavor Society."[8]

Just a few weeks later, on March 23, 1904, Maud's nephew, Chester, son of Walter and Lida Hoyle, died of "creeping paralysis" which is now known as Werdig-

Hoffman Disease, a form of muscular dystrophy. Chester was only fourteen months old.

This must have been a very difficult time for Maud and her family; yet, there is no indication that Maud's faith ever waned. In the year or two before these tragedies, Maud began a formal study for Sunday School teachers through the International Sunday School Association (ISSA). The ISSA was an interdenominational organization established to coordinate religious instruction in Sunday Schools by developing a uniform curriculum. It also helped to standardize teacher training for Sunday School teachers.[9]

The course that Maud took was probably a two-year program devoted to the study of the Bible and a "general study of Sunday-school organization and management and a study of the essential principles and methods of teaching."[10] The program included written examinations and the granting of a diploma at graduation of those who made "a grade of not less than seventy percent."[11] It is not known if this was a correspondence course or one taught in different locales offered by various associations affiliated with the ISSA. Whatever the case, Maud's vita indicates that she graduated from the International Sunday School Association on March 31, 1905, a year before she entered seminary to become a minister in the United Brethren Church.

The United Brethren

Before reviewing Maud's time in seminary, it might be helpful to learn more about this denomination that had given Maud the foundation of her faith—a deep, abiding belief in Jesus Christ as Son of God and Savior of this world, and guiding principles for the way she lived her life. There are a number of books written about the United Brethren Church.[12] What appears here is a brief summary, highlighting its history and doctrine.

As noted earlier, the United Brethren in Christ Church was founded by Philip Otterbein, a German Reformed pastor. In 1767, Otterbein heard the Mennonite minister Martin Boehm preach in Lancaster, Pennsylvania, and realized that despite some differences, they were "brethren" in regard to the basics of their faith. They both preached that religion was more than ritual. Instead, they emphasized that God's grace leads to a transformed life and that it was imperative for Christians to have an intimate daily relationship with Christ. Eventually, the two decided to come together and form the United Brethren in Christ Church (commonly referred to just as "United Brethren"). This new denomination was formally launched in 1800 in Frederick, Maryland, and was one of the first denominations entirely originating in this country.

15. Philip Otterbein

16. Martin Boehm

The United Brethren Church had approximately 25,000 members by 1841. The church grew considerably over the next few decades and by the late 1800s, there were over 200,000 members. However, because of opposition to proposed changes in the Church's constitution, an estimated 10,000 to 20,000 members of the Church withdrew their membership in 1889 and formed a separate organization. This group was led by Bishop Milton Wright (father of the famed Orville and Wilbur). Until 1946 both groups operated under the name Church of the United Brethren in Christ, with the smaller group designated as "Old Constitution" and the majority group as the "New Constitution." (Maud belonged to the New Constitution church.) In 1946, the larger New Constitution church (with over 433,000 members) merged with the Evangelical Association, a church begun by Jacob Albright in 1803. The newly formed organization was known as the Evangelical United Brethren Church (EUB). This change in name allowed the "Old Constitution" church to be known just as the "United Brethren Church in Christ." This denomination still exists today with about 500 churches in eighteen countries. In 1968, the Evangelical United Brethren Church merged with the Methodist Church (USA) to form the United Methodist Church.

17. Jacob Albright

From the beginning, the doctrine and methods of work of the United Brethren were very similar to that of the Methodist Church. However, the Methodists focused more on preaching to the English descendants while the United Brethren concentrated on reaching German-speaking people in Pennsylvania, Maryland, Virginia, and Ohio. Indeed, the early United Brethren churches conducted their services in German through much of the first half of the 19th century and some continued its use even into the early 1900s.

The United Brethren believed in the Trinity (God the Father, God the Son, and God, the Holy Ghost), that Jesus Christ is the Savior of all who believe in him, and that the Bible is the word of God. They put a strong emphasis on God's grace and the need for a personal commitment to Christ. Additionally, they believed in ethical living (including the abstinence of tobacco and alcohol), good will, equality, and justice. While they believed that their salvation came by faith, and not by their works, they also believed that a true and living faith would produce good works and a commitment to fight for social justice (equal economic, political and social rights and opportunities).

In 1821, the Church denounced slavery and would not allow slave owners to become members. It should be noted that except for Maryland and Virginia, the United Brethren churches at that time were in the northern states. In 1847, the United Brethren founded Otterbein College (now Otterbein University) in Westerville, Ohio. It was one of the first American institutions of higher learning to admit females and persons of color as students on an equal basis as white, male students. Additionally, Otterbein College was probably the first college in the country (and possibly the world) to have women as fully accepted faculty members.

Denouncing the social ills of the world and working for change became a strong focus of the Church in the early Twentieth Century. In 1909, the Church adopted a social creed which delineated what the United Brethren stood for.[13] Among the causes listed were:

> Equal rights and complete justice for all men in all conditions of life;
> Protection of the family (e.g., uniform divorce laws, proper housing);
> Fullest possible development of every child;
> Abolition of child labor;
> Abatement and prevention of poverty;
> Protection of the worker from dangerous machinery;
> Suitable provision for old age;
> A living wage as a minimum in every industry and for the highest wage that each industry can afford

Some of the results of the Church's social conscience included the United Brethren opening orphanages, a home for the elderly, and a home for retired ministers.

The United Brethren were also evangelical in that they believed in sharing the Gospel with those in need, preaching the good news of Jesus' love and grace. They began supporting missionaries at home and abroad. In this country, their notable mission work was with the Spanish Americans in New Mexico and the underprivileged in Kentucky. Foreign missions included locations in China, Japan, the Philippines, Puerto Rico, and, of course, Sierra Leone.

It was in this denomination, the United Brethren in Christ, that Maud was confirmed and made a commitment to serve God by becoming a minister in the church. She was twenty-five when she entered Union Biblical Seminary in 1906.

News of the Times

1898 – The Spanish-American War begins.

1898 – The Philippines declare independence from Spain.

1900 – The Boxer Rebellion begins in China.

1900 – Average age at death in the United States is 47.

1901 – U. S. President McKinley assassinated, and Theodore Roosevelt becomes President.

1901 – Queen Victoria of the United Kingdom dies after a reign of nearly 64 years.

1903 – The Wright Brothers conduct the world's first successful flight.

1904 – St. Louis World Fair held between April 30–December 1, attracts notable visitors John Phillip Sousa, Scott Joplin, Helen Keller, and T. S. Eliot.

1905 – First major polio epidemic takes place in Sweden.

1905 – Einstein publishes his paper on the theory of relativity ($E=mc^2$).

A few of the active artists, musicians, and writers at this time: Matisse, Monet, Debussy, Puccini, Ravel, O. Henry, Upton Sinclair, H.G. Wells.

Chapter Three:
Preparing for the Road Ahead

Your word is a lamp for my feet,
a light on my path.
—Psalm 119:105 (NIV)

Union Biblical Seminary, located in Dayton, Ohio, opened in 1871 and was the only United Brethren seminary in the country.[14] In 1906 (the year that Maud entered the Seminary), John and Mary Bonebrake gave Union Biblical Seminary land in Kansas valued at $86,400. In return, in 1909, the seminary changed its name to Bonebrake Theological Seminary in honor of the six great uncles of John Bonebrake who had been United Brethren preachers. Maud was in the first graduating class under the newly named seminary. Much later, in 1954, the Evangelical School of Theology located in Reading, Pennsylvania, merged with Bonebrake to form the United Theological Seminary. UTS still exists today (now as a United Methodist seminary) and is located in Trotwood, Ohio, just a few miles from Dayton. It is also the home of the Center for the Evangelical United Brethren Heritage, which proved to be a wonderful resource in researching Maud's life in the seminary and later in the mission field.

One family legend about Maud was that she was the first woman to graduate from the Seminary. However, this is one story that proved not to be true. The Seminary, in fact, began accepting women as students in 1873, with the first woman graduating in 1883. It is interesting to note, though, that the United Brethren Church did not officially accept or ordain women ministers until 1889. In thinking about this, it is important to remember that this was still more than thirty years before women had the right to vote in this country. Prior to 1889, few other major denominations in the United States officially ordained women. Those that allowed women to be ordained include the Quakers, the Salvation Army, Disciples of Christ, Unitarians, and the United Church of Christ. Also of interest is that it was not until 1956 that the predecessors of the United Methodist Church and the Presbyterian Church (USA) began ordaining women. The Lutheran Church in America (now ELCA) didn't accept female ministers until 1970. Of course, there are still a number of denominations that do not allow women to be ordained.[15] So while Maud was not the first woman to graduate from Bonebrake Seminary, clearly women were still in the minority, both at the Seminary and in the ministry.

What was life in the Seminary like for Maud? Starting with the admissions requirement, we learn from the 1906 *Seminary Bulletin* that "Applicants for admission into the Seminary must be members in good standing of some evangelical church. They must have written testimonials of a prudent and discreet deportment and that they possess competent talents for the ministry." Further, applicants were expected to be college graduates "unless they have otherwise qualified themselves to pursue with advantage the prescribed course."[16] Since Maud hadn't even graduated from high school, the seminary obviously found her to be "otherwise qualified."

There were two courses of study for the ministry. The "Regular Course" for those who had previously attended college or who had studied several subjects including Greek, logic, psychology, and moral science. Those who had not taken the preparatory studies were enrolled in the "English Course." The Regular Course generally took two years to complete while the English Course (in which Maud was enrolled) took three years.

The 1907 *Seminary Bulletin* states "the English Course differs from the regular course in two particulars: 1. As preparatory to it, students are required to pursue, in residence, courses in Ethics, Logic, General History, and General Psychology. 2. Instead of the exegetical work in Hebrew and Greek (Old Testament and New Testament), courses are required in English exegesis. Otherwise the courses are identical."[17]

The Scheme of Instruction for the English Course included the following:

Junior Year
Bible (introduction, harmony and interpretation of the Gospels; Revelation; taught by Dr. Faust)
Systematic Theology (including comparative religion; taught by Dr. Drury)
History (the ancient church, medieval civilization, Old Testament history; taught by Dr. Faust)
Practical (vocal expression, writing and preaching sermons, sociology; taught by Prof. Clippinger, Dr. Drury, and Dr. Landis)

Middle Year
Bible (emphasis on Epistles; taught by Dr. Faust and Dr. Landis)
Systematic Theology (natural religion, dogmatic theology; taught by Dr. Drury)
History (church and general; taught by Dr. Faust)
Practical (history of preaching, sermon building, liturgies, missions, sociology; taught by Prof. Clippinger, Dr. Drury, and Dr. Landis)

Senior Year
Bible (Old Testament; taught by Dr. Faust)
Systematic Theology (theology of Christ and the Christian church, salvation, and the end of the ages; taught by Dr. Drury)
History (history and governance of the United Brethren Church; taught by Dr. Faust)
Practical (Sunday School pedagogy and administration, psychology, child study, pastoral theology, homiletics, public preaching; taught by Prof. Clippinger, Dr. Landis, and Dr. Funkhouser)

Again, from the 1906 *Seminary Bulletin*, we learn that "There is no charge for tuition or room rent."[18] (Wouldn't today's students love to read that!) The Seminary building provided "first-class accommodations" for the students. Rooms were "well-furnished with carpets, wardrobes, bookcases, beds, chairs, mirrors, and all essentials for comfort" and were "heated by the best modern methods." There were also provisions within the building for bathing without additional charge.

There was an annual incidental fee of $20, which covered furnishing, heating, and care of the room. Students who lived off campus were charged an incidental fee of $3, which allowed them the use of the reception room, the library, and bathrooms! Students took their meals in the private homes of families and generally paid between $2.25–$3.00 per week. With textbooks for the entire course costing between $30–$40, the total annual expense to attend the Seminary, "including washing," was between $125–$150.

The Seminary's library was "selected with wisdom, and adapted to the needs of the theological student" and had a "regularly appointed librarian." Additionally, there was a reading room in the Seminary building which contained the leading religious and secular periodicals of the day.

The Rev. George A. Funkhouser, who was one of two full-time professors when the Seminary opened in 1871, wrote his reminiscences for the fortieth anniversary of Bonebrake Seminary.[19] He mentions that in 1882, the Seminary acquired a bell that had been brought across the Allegheny Mountains for a United Brethren Church in Germantown (Ohio). This bell was placed in a tower at the Seminary and "for many years was rung at five o'clock every morning for students to arise... and again at nine o'clock at night for students to cease work and go to bed, and many obeyed its motherly admonitions." Funkhouser also said that "for many years printed rules were put into the hands of every students—printed on paper, not on erasable tablets of the mind, indicating what was required in order to get most benefit out of his stay in the Seminary." There are no records of the list of rules or any indication of whether the bell was used when Maud was there. However, it is safe to say that it is likely that Maud and her classmates led fairly structured lives while at Bonebrake.

In his remembrances, Dr. Funkhouser also mentions that it was important to pay tribute to the wives of the professors for their part in making the Seminary what is was. The wives opened "their homes, and hearts as well, day and night, to the incoming students, giving warm welcome, cheering the homesick by motherly solicitude and motherly delicacies when too ill to leave their rooms...."

Among Maud's artifacts, is a poem, in her handwriting, that described a little of life at Bonebrake. It could be sung to the tune of "Yankee Doodle" and begins[20]:

> When first I came into the Sem
> I hadn't any warning
> That men and boys outnumbered us
> So far. Twas quite alarming.
> For I was so afraid of them
> Would scarce pause to hear them
> When they would pass the time of day
> I dreaded to be near them.
>
> But then I found some other girls
> Who felt the same as I did
> We pledged each other to support
> And 'gainst the men we sided
> But that was long ago
> And now, we know them better,
> We judge them much more leniently...

Indeed, in Maud's graduating class, there were twelve men and four women, Maud, Adda D. May, Etta Odle (who would serve as a missionary in Sierra Leone), and Mable Drury (the daughter of the faculty member, Dr. Drury who taught Systematic Theology). Below is a photo of the four women; Maud is on the far left.

18. Women in 1909 Bonebrake Seminary Graduating Class

The poem goes on to echo Dr. Funkhouser's praise for the faculty wives:

> Now there is Mrs. Funkhouser,
> She truly is a mother,
> To all these grown-up boys and girls,
> We would not have another.
> And Mrs. Drury kind and sweet,
> The mother of our Mable
> To tell of her rare qualities
> We really are not able.

> Then Mrs. Landis, Mrs. Faust,
> So oft they work together,
> Are in and out on our behalf,
> In every kind of weather.
> Like sisters true to us are they,
> We could not do without them.

After describing a scrumptious turkey dinner which the wives had prepared, the poem ends:

> Hurrah for good old Bonebrake Sem.
> Hurrah for all our teachers,
> Hurrah for all the wives, of course,
> For they are lovely creatures.

Beginning in 1907, students were required to write a thesis before graduating. Maud entitled her thesis *Practical Christianity*.[21] In her first paragraph, she wrote that "the test of true religion is its power to help, to relieve suffering, and to transform lives." She then proceeded to give a history and accounting of various Christian organizations and the work that they did (providing food and shelter for the destitute, friendship to the prisoners, homes for deserted children, medical help for those injured by natural disasters or war, etc.). The organizations that she discussed include the Red Cross, Salvation Army, Sisters of Charity, and the YMCA, among others. She also included a section about the work of missionaries where the "gospel of a clean shirt went side by side with that of repentance." It is clear from reading this eighty-six-page hand-written thesis that she had visited a number of sites to see the work first-hand, including a Salvation Army shelter and an insane asylum.

In the last part of her thesis, Maud wrote about how many churches have followed the example of John Wesley (founder of the Methodist Church), who ministered to the poor in so many ways. She ends by saying that these practices are attainable by everyone—in their homes, in their daily work and businesses, and in the narrow circle of their acquaintances.

> The substantial essence of religion does not consist in deep experiences, but in duty performed.... In the mind of every thoughtful man there stands out as never before the one ideal of this religion, the Man of Sorrows, he who said "Thou shalt love the Lord thy God with all the heart and thy neighbor as thyself."

A transcription of her thesis is in Part Two of this book.

In 1908, Maud applied for her Quarterly Conference license which would allow her to preach. (The Quarterly Conference represented the church at the local level.) Applicants for the Quarterly Conference License had to express "their purpose to make the ministry their life work" and give evidence "of their call, religious experience, soundness of doctrine, and attachment to the Church...." If they had not completed specific courses, they were required to pass an examination. Persons divorced, except on scriptural grounds, were not approved, nor were those who used tobacco in any form.[22]

Maud was granted the Quarterly Conference License on June 11, 1908, and Rev. C W. Kurtz, the presiding elder, signed her certificate. A year later, on May 8, 1909, Maud graduated from Bonebrake.

The 1909 annual session of the Miami Conference was held at the First United Brethren Church in Dayton Ohio. On August 25, Maud appeared before the Com-

19. Maud's Graduation Photo, 1909

mittee on Elders' Orders regarding her application to become ordained. The minutes state "...it is with great pleasure that we make the following report:

1. Miss Hoyle has completed a course of study in Bonebrake Theological Seminary.
2. She contemplates further preparation for foreign missionary work by taking a course in medicine at the Starling Medical College, Columbus, Ohio.
3. She was clear and definite in her answers to the questions per Discipline. We therefore recommend that she be ordained to the gospel ministry."[23]

The following day was one of the most joyful days of her life, for that was when she was ordained and became the Reverend Maud E. Hoyle. She then received her Annual Conference License, signed by Bishop Belle, authorizing her to administer the sacraments (baptism and communion) of the Church.

News of the Times

1906 – A San Francisco Earthquake kills 3,000.
1906 – Excavation for the Panama Canal begins.
1908 – U. S. banks begin to shut their doors as economic depression takes over.
1908 – Model T Ford is introduced.
1908 – The Chicago Cubs win the World Series.
1908 – William Howard Taft elected President.
1909 – Orville Wright introduces the airplane into the U.S. Army.

A few of the active artists, musicians, and writers at this time: Matisse, Kipling, Mahler.

Chapter Four:
Plant My Feet on Higher Ground

But they that wait upon the LORD
shall renew their strength;
they shall mount up with wings as eagles;
they shall run, and not be weary;
and they shall walk, and not faint.
—Isaiah 40:31 (KJV)

After her ordination in 1909, Maud returned to Springfield and helped with chores at home. She also returned to the Lagonda United Brethren Church where she was immediately put to work assisting the pastor in various ways, including giving some sermons. The earliest dated sermon of hers in her artifacts is one that she gave at a Sunday evening service on February 20, 1910. It is entitled *Salvation*[24] and based on Romans 10:13: "Whoever shall call upon the name of the Lord shall be saved." A copy of this sermon is in Part Two.

Most of what is known about the other work she did for the church at this time comes from Maud's own account of the history of the Columbus Avenue United Brethren Church.[25] Information in the following paragraphs is taken from this history. (The complete history can be found in Part Two.)

Prior to Maud attending seminary, the Lagonda UB Church sponsored a Sunday School held at the old Benson Schoolhouse. This was a way to minister to the families who lived closer to the schoolhouse than to the church. Since most of the people who lived in this area had to walk to church or had a buggy that wasn't large enough for the entire family, it was often difficult to attend regularly. People from all denominations were welcome at the Sunday School and it thrived for several years. However, it was eventually discontinued because there were not enough teachers. Once Maud returned from seminary, she was asked to help organize cottage prayer meetings. These were held on Tuesday evenings in homes of people who lived in the Columbus Avenue neighborhood.

Eventually those attending these prayer meetings began to express a desire to have a church built closer to them. They asked Maud to find a way to make it happen. Maud had to have been a strong and determined woman. She was young (twenty-nine), single, and petite, and just two years out of seminary. Yet, she was not intimidated by the task she had before her. It is obvious that she had earned the trust and respect of the people in the community and the church.

Maud presented the request to the Quarterly Conference on July 15, 1911. Rev. C. W. Kurtz, the presiding elder of the conference and Dr. Klinefelter, pastor of the Lagonda church, selected a committee of three men to study the request and then to give their advice at the next Quarterly Conference. Their report was favorable, and they were then asked to select a suitable site to build the new church. The committee found a lot

20. Surveyor's Description of lot for the new Columbus Avenue Church

located close to the intersection of Pump House Road and Columbus Avenue and purchased it from Harry Kohl, Sr. for $190.

The trustees and the finance committee members for the new church were selected at the Quarterly Conference held on January 27, 1912, at the Lagonda United Brethren Church. Maud was on the finance committee. It is worth noting that the five trustees were all male, but the three finance committee members were all women.

Groundbreaking for the Columbus Avenue United Brethren Church took place on March 4, 1912. The "short, but impressive ceremony" started with the hymn "Lord, Plant My Feet on Higher Ground."[26]

> 1. I'm pressing on the upward way,
> New heights I'm gaining every day;
> Still praying as I'm onward bound,
> "Lord, plant my feet on higher ground."
>
> **Chorus:**
> Lord, lift me up and let me stand,
> By faith, on Heaven's table land,
> A higher plane than I have found;
> Lord, plant my feet on higher ground.
>
> 2. My heart has no desire to stay
> Where doubts arise and fears dismay;
> Though some may dwell where those abound,
> My prayer, my aim, is higher ground.
>
> 3. I want to live above the world,
> Though Satan's darts at me are hurled;
> For faith has caught the joyful sound,
> The song of saints on higher ground.
>
> 4. I want to scale the utmost height
> And catch a gleam of glory bright;
> But still I'll pray till Heav'n I've found,
> "Lord, plant my feet on higher ground."

The service continued with Rev. Ferris, the new pastor of Lagonda United Brethren Church, giving the sermon based on Psalm 127:1 which is "Unless the LORD builds the house, the builders labor in vain. Unless the LORD watches over the city, the guards stand watch in vain." Maud was given the honor of turning over the first shovelful of dirt. The ceremony ended with the hymn, "I Want to Be a Worker" and a prayer given by Maud.

21. Groundbreaking of the Columbus Avenue United Brethren Church

Later that month, on March 20, the cornerstone was laid. Members filled a jar with various items of the day which was placed in the cornerstone. Some of the items were a Bible, the history of the church written by Maud, a message to future pastors written by Rev. Ferris, and some coins. In writing about the ceremony held that day, Maud states, "The church never was more earnest or deeply spiritual."

The church was built largely through the donated labor of members and friends of the church. Although member James Truman is listed as the official overseer of the work, Maud undoubtedly followed each step of the process closely, convincing people to volunteer, and offering encouragement when needed. The workers were certainly inspired by her determination and faith in God.

The church was one story with a belfry bell tower, basement, furnace, and seating for 250. The total cost to complete the building was $2,500. When it opened, it was lit with kerosene lamps placed at each window and a large chandelier in the ceiling held several more lamps. Later, the church converted to gas lamps and eventually electricity was added, and a parsonage was built in 1918. Mrs. Crawford, a member of the Lagonda church, donated an organ.

Maud, officially appointed as the first pastor of this church, led its first service (an evening prayer meeting) on August 27, 1912. The church began with fifty-one charter members. Among the charter members was

22. Columbus Avenue United Brethren Church, circa 1912 with hitching posts in front

Maud's mother, Ida. While her father, Stephen, attended this church, he was Catholic and had promised his mother that he would not convert while she was alive. As it turned out, Stephen died before his mother and he never was a member of his daughter's church.

Shortly after the church opened its doors, Maud organized a Sunday School with 134 members; a Young People's Society of Christian Endeavor with thirty-four members; and thirty-seven members in the Ladies Aid Society which hosted dinners and other fundraisers for the church. The dedication ceremony was held on November 3, 1912.

January 3, 1915, was a special day for the church, as the trustees held a ceremony to burn the mortgage for the property and building. After the flames died down, it was discovered that one small piece of charred paper remained, and this piece had one word on it—"paid."

There is an addendum to Maud's history of the church. This addendum was written by Rev. A. J. Furstenberger, who was pastor of the church from 1930–1935. He wrote:

> In the previous account of the organization, written by Miss Maud Hoyle, she has in her reserve and modesty practically submerged the fact that she is the promoter of the Columbus Avenue U. B. Chapel. Since this is so, the undersigned feels that this notation should be added:
>
> Mr. Wilson Hinman, a charter member had written this—
>
> "History of Columbus Avenue U B Chapel and tribute to its Founder, Miss Maud Hoyle, for had it not been for the untiring efforts of the latter, there probably would be no history to write.
>
> "As it is well known that from the beginning of time God raised up men and women to carry out His program, and assuredly as He laid His hand on Philip William Otterbein and Martin Boehm, so did He call Miss Maud Hoyle to further His Kingdom by founding Columbus Avenue U B Chapel."
>
> The church asked Miss Hoyle to make up this record, instructing Wilson Hinman to prepare an introductory, but Maud submerged this, because it referred to herself.[27]

This accolade for Maud's leadership in the building of the church had been noted earlier in the 1913 minutes of the Annual Conference. In the information about the dedication of the Columbus Avenue church, it was noted that "the pastor, Miss Maud Hoyle, deserves great credit for this work and the splendid condition of the church at this time."[28]

In 1914, Maud's official ministerial status changed from "Local Minister" to "Active Itinerate." In the United Brethren Church, there were several classifications of the ministry. "Local ministers" were ordained annual conference preachers who for any reason were without ministerial employment or who had not yet been admitted to the "itinerancy." To become an "itinerant" one usually had to work for several years under the direction of a conference superintendent or have been engaged in special work recognized and approved by the annual conference. Itinerants were active ministers, appointed for a one-year term and subject to reappointment and location reassignment. They had to agree "to be adaptable to the form of service to which he was appointed or elected, and literally to travel to and within the area where his service was to be given."[29]

Maud served as pastor of the Columbus Avenue church from 1912–1917. During the first year, eleven new members joined the church. Sunday School attendance increased by forty-five and the Christian Endeavor Society had fifteen new members. By 1917, the membership of the church doubled to more than one hundred. The church also held at least two evangelistic services during the time Maud was pastor. The first one held in 1912 lasted two weeks and resulted in nine conversions. The second one conducted in 1916 brought twenty-three new converts. We do not have any record of Maud's specific day-to-day work with the church other than what was spelled out in the *Discipline* of the United Brethren Church. According to this document, the duties of pastors were

> to preach Christ crucified; to organize churches..., converse with the members on their spiritual condition; administer relief, strengthen and direct those that are afflicted of labor under temptations; animate the indolent; endeavor as much as possible to edify and instruct all in faith..., and visit the sick.[30]

Knowing what we do about Maud's commitment to God, we can be assured that she fulfilled her duties with love and compassion.

We do have a handful of her handwritten sermons that she preached. These are in quite fragile condition, with some missing pages. Most are undated.

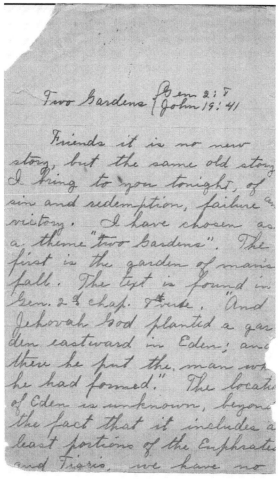

23. Page from Sermon, "Two Gardens"

Additionally, there were several sermon outlines found in her Bible. Here is one:

24. Sermon Outline

The overall message in Maud's sermons was the good news of salvation by grace through the belief in Jesus Christ. She spoke often of God's abiding love and forgiveness. Transcriptions of four of her sermons can be found in Part Two. Reading Maud's own words will provide greater insight into her beliefs.

One of her sermons, however, does deserve special mention. It is important because it was the "first regular sermon" given in the Columbus Avenue Chapel when it opened. It is entitled *The Love of Christ to His People* and the text is found in John 15:9, "As the Father has loved me, so have I loved you. Now remain in my love."

In this sermon, Maud encouraged her listeners to rejoice and receive God's blessings of love—pardon, peace, righteousness, joy, and immortality. She then exhorted her congregation to put their Christianity into practice saying "Men of the world do not read God's word to find out what is religion. They look to the life and conduct of those who profess to believe it. A good life is the most powerful preaching." These ideas are reminiscent of the thesis she wrote in Seminary.

This sermon is also important because it was read at the last service held in the Columbus Avenue Church before closing its doors and merging with the Brighton United Methodist Church on December 27, 2009.

Church has last service

Columbus Avenue United Methodist's congregation to join Brighton UMC.

By Bridgette Outten
Staff Writer

SPRINGFIELD — Columbus Avenue United Methodist Church ended in the same way that it began more than 97 years ago — with a message of love.

The Rev. Richard Johnson was able to unearth the first sermon preached at Columbus Avenue, which began in 1912 as United Brethren Church. Johnson read the words of the church's founder and first pastor, the Rev. Maud Hoyle, at the last service Sunday, Dec. 27. The church is closing its doors at 2967 Columbus Ave. to merge with Brighton United Methodist Church.

With the unusual job of being a female pastor, Hoyle titled her sermon "The Love of Christ to His People" all those years ago.

"We've done what she said in that first sermon," said Johnson, speaking of Hoyle. "Christ was concerned that His love was passed. We did that."

United Brethren became Evangelical United Brethren before joining the Methodist church in the 1970s.

A plaque dedicated to the memory of the Rev. Maud Hoyle, the first pastor of the 97-year-old Columbus Avenue United Methodist Church, hangs near the entrance Sunday, Dec. 27.

There were 42 members when Johnson became pastor in 1993, he said, but membership dwindled over the years, and now the church has only 10 members.

"It just seems that people don't go to the smaller churches anymore," said Johnson, who will also pastor the merged church until a replacement can be found.

The members who stayed are saddened by the loss of their church.

Robert Teets' loss was compounded by the death of his twin brother, Roger, last week. His parents were longtime members of Columbus Avenue.

"It hurts," Robert Teets, 81, said.

It is a sentiment echoed by 83-year-old Kathleen Adams, 89-year-old Irmal Grubbs, 81-year-old Edna Kirby and musician Dorothy Setty, plus others with years of memories in the church.

Some of the elderly members will not be joining Brighton, but they all go forward with that same message of love.

"I send you from this place to continue what started with the love of God to many people," Johnson said during his benediction in a voice thick with tears.

Staff writer Tom Stafford contributed to this report.

Contact this reporter at (937) 328-0374 or boutten@coxohio.com.

25. From the Springfield News-Sun, December 27, 2009

As noted above, Maud served as pastor of this church for five years. She left this position because she again felt the nudge for her to take another step towards fulfilling her calling of becoming a medical missionary. She did not attend the Starling Medical College as she had originally planned, probably because of lack of funds. Instead, she entered the Springfield Nurse's Training School in 1917. She was thirty-six years old.

News of the Times

1910 – The average U.S. wage is less than $15/week and the nation faces large amounts of unemployment.

1912 – Over 1500 passengers drown in the sinking of the Titanic.

1912 – Woodrow Wilson elected President.

1913 – Protests for women's suffrage continue in London and Washington, D.C.

1914 – World War I begins in Europe.

1914 – Panama Canal opens.

1916 – Norman Rockwell illustration first appears on Saturday Evening Post cover.

1917 – The U.S. enters World War I, declaring war on Germany.

A few of the active artists, musicians, and writers at this time: Chagall, Picasso, Irving Berlin, Stravinsky, Ravel, Robert Frost, Kipling.

Chapter Five:
Another Step Forward

> *I will instruct you and teach you*
> *concerning the path you should walk;*
> *I will direct you with my eye.*
> —Psalm 32:8 (ISV)

The modern era of professionally trained nurses began in 1860 when Florence Nightingale opened the world's first secular school of nursing. While this movement began in England, it soon traveled to the United States. Eventually hospitals began setting up their own nursing schools, which allowed women to train closer to home. Another advantage of the hospital-run nursing programs was that students could gain clinical experience in addition to the formal "book learning." In 1900, there were 432 nursing schools in the United States. By 1920, that number had increased to 1,755.[31] One of the schools begun during this time was the one in Springfield that Maud attended.

Mitchell-Thomas Hospital, built in 1887, was the first hospital in Springfield and had eighteen beds.[32] In 1904, philanthropist John Snyder left a bequest of $100,000 to build a new hospital. The new facility, named the Springfield City Hospital, was located on Selma Road and it stood high on a hill about forty feet above the street level. It had a capacity for 120 patients in either private rooms or wards. The hospital had an ambulance service and a free dispensary. It was in this new facility that the hospital began the Springfield Nurses' Training School.

At the time that Maud attended the Nursing School, there were approximately forty-five students in the pro-

26. Springfield City Hospital, circa 1910

gram and they lived in the cottages behind the hospital.[33] Some of the courses offered were taught by the faculty in the chemistry department at Springfield High School. Other than this, little is known specifically about the Springfield Nurses' Training School when Maud attended. However, the 1923 study, *Nursing and Nursing Education in the United States and the National League of Nursing Education's Standard Curriculum*[34], provide a wealth of information about similar programs from which we can get a glimpse of Maud's life as a student nurse.

The course of study at most hospital-run nursing schools took three calendar years with one month vacation each year. It was the practice at that time to charge nothing for tuition, room, board, or uniforms. Some schools also gave students a stipend. However, in exchange, students were required to work in the hospital, often over fifty hours per week. Because of the need to staff the hospital seven days a week, it was customary for student nurses to work five full days (8–10 hours/day shift or 12 hours/night shift) plus two half days; thus, never having a full day off. This was in addition to attending classes and studying.

The work that student nurses performed, particularly in their first year, involved many menial tasks (disinfecting bedpans, washing stained linens, bed-making, bathing and feeding patients, etc.). It was felt that students had to do

> enough of certain tasks, naturally perhaps distasteful or repulsive, to get finally rid of whatever inhibitions or repugnances she may feel towards them. The nurse must have no shrinking nerves, no repugnances, no inhibitions; if she retains them, she had better seek her vocation elsewhere.[35]

Juniors and seniors had more advanced duties including performing irrigations, catheterizations, drawing blood, operating room assistance, and care of obstetrical patients. Students received experience working in all the major areas—medical, surgical, children's, and obstetrics. Some schools also offered training in more specialized areas such as nervous and mental disorders, contagious diseases, eye, ear, nose, and throat. This practical learning most often was 90% of a nurse's education.

The other 10% of the program dealt more with the academic side of nursing education with emphasis on the basic sciences. First year students would usually take classes in anatomy and physiology, chemistry, bacteriology, bandaging, and cooking and nutrition, along with the study of social and ethical principles of nursing. Juniors would study communicable diseases nursing in diseases of infants and children, obstetrical and gynecological nursing, and operating room technique. The senior level courses included subjects such as nursing in mental and nervous disorders, public sanitation, emergency nursing, and public health nursing.

Maud was in nurse's training from 1917–1920. It was during this time that the 1918 Influenza Epidemic hit this country, killing more than twenty-one million people. More than 5,000 in Springfield were struck by this illness. Undoubtedly, Maud's experience included caring for many of them. While she was not living at home during these years, she also probably spent as much time as possible caring for her father who had an unknown illness for several months before he passed away on December 11, 1919.

27. Maud, circa 1920

After spending three years absorbing all that she could about being a nurse, Maud graduated on May 20, 1920. Her life's path had taken her from being a truck farmer's daughter to becoming an ordained minister, and then a trained nurse. Now, at the age of forty, she was at last ready for the biggest step in her journey, one which would allow her to achieve her life's goal of being a medical missionary.

News of the Times

1918 – The Influenza Pandemic begins and continues for two years, infecting over 500 million people worldwide.

1918 – World War I ends with armistice signed by Germany and Allies on November 11.

1919 – The Eighteenth Amendment, also known as the Prohibition Amendment, takes effect.

1919 – Mahatma Gandhi begins his non–violent resistance of British control of India.

1919 – Treaty of Versailles is signed and establishes the League of Nations.

1920 – The Nineteenth Amendment grants women the right to vote.

1920 – Warren G. Harding elected President.

1920 – Babe Ruth signs with the New York Yankees.

1920 – Prohibition begins in the United States.

A few of the active artists, musicians, and writers at this time: Klee, Matisse, Gershwin, Ravel, Prokofiev, Carl Sandburg, James Whitcomb Riley.

Chapter Six: Go!

He said to them, "Go into all the world and preach the gospel to all creation."
— Mark 16:15 (NIV)

Sometime early in 1920, Maud contacted the United Brethren's Foreign Missionary Society in Dayton to express her desire to serve as a medical missionary. In response, she received an application form and a copy of the *Missionary Manual*, which listed the qualifications for becoming a missionary along with general information regarding terms of service, travel allowances, and other expectations. Two editions of this work, one published in 1894 and the second in 1924, were in effect while Maud was an active missionary.[36]

The general requirements for missionaries were similar in the two editions: candidates needed to have a high standard of ability and character, to have felt "divinely called" to a life of self-sacrifice and humble service, to provide a letter from a physician stating the candidate's physical condition, and to have taken a course in Bible study.

The application to become a missionary included twenty-eight questions. In addition to ones about church membership and Bible study, there were also a number of questions related to the candidate's temperament, physical and mental health.[37] Candidates also needed to interview with Board officers in Dayton, Ohio.

For those who were accepted as missionaries, the

United Brethren Board of Missions would pay the expenses of the journey to the mission station and the return trip home after a term of service. It was hoped that the missionary's home church and/or friends would help pay for the necessary clothing and supplies as required for a different climate. If that weren't possible, the Mission Board would provide a grant of $100 for this purpose.

The 1894 edition of the *Manual* included an additional requirement that all ladies have "some experience in teaching and nursing." It further stated that ladies "must not be less than twenty-five or more than forty years of age." Gentlemen, however, were not required to have the additional experience in teaching or medicine. Also, men could serve until they were forty-five. The age requirement in the 1924 *Manual* did not distinguish between men and women; however, it stated that "all ordinary appointments should not be above thirty years of age."[38]

Deviation from these rules would be considered if one possessed a "thorough intellectual training, with a facility in acquiring languages, and a remarkable ability for Christian work."[39] Apparently, Maud was not deterred by the criteria since she was thirty-nine when she applied. She had been accepted into seminary without the prerequisite of an undergraduate degree and she remained confident that she would be accepted into her life's calling as a missionary. Her intelligence and determination, along with her academic credentials led the Mission Board to conclude that Maud did indeed possess "a remarkable ability for Christian work" and in August 1920, she was accepted and told to prepare for her assignment in Rotifunk, Sierra Leone, West Africa. Plans were made for her to sail by the end of the year.

While she must have been thrilled with the assignment, her mother undoubtedly felt both pride in her daughter as well as some anxiety about Maud going to a far-off land. What was the country like? What were the people like? What kind of food did they have? What protection was there against the heat and insects? What did she need to do to prepare for this next venture in her life? Maud and her mother began learning all they could about Sierra Leone. Some they learned through reading books and articles in *The Evangel*, the monthly magazine published by the United Brethren Women's Missionary Society. They probably also talked with missionaries who had returned home. Certainly, the Board of Missions would have also provided counsel and admonitions. The following paragraphs contain a greatly condensed overview of what Maud and Ida likely discovered about Sierra Leone.[40]

Sierra Leone

The West African country of Sierra Leone is bordered on the north and east by Guinea (formerly French Guinea), on the south by Liberia, and on the west by the Atlantic Ocean. It is roughly circular in shape and has 27,925 square miles, which is a little smaller than South Carolina. "Portuguese voyagers in the mid-fifteenth century named the peninsula *Serra Lyoa* from the wild-looking, leonine mountains."[41] Over time, the name changed to Sierra Leone.

These mountains cover twenty-five miles and are 4,000 to 6,000 feet high. Sierra Leone also has swamp lands by the coast, a plateau in the eastern part of the country, lowland interior plains, and rain-forest plains in the south. The climate is tropical with two major seasons: the rainy season from May to November when it rains almost daily and the dry season from December to May, which includes harmattan, when cool, dry winds blow in off the Sahara Desert. Generally, conditions are hot and humid year-round. Temperatures range from 70° F to over 100° F.

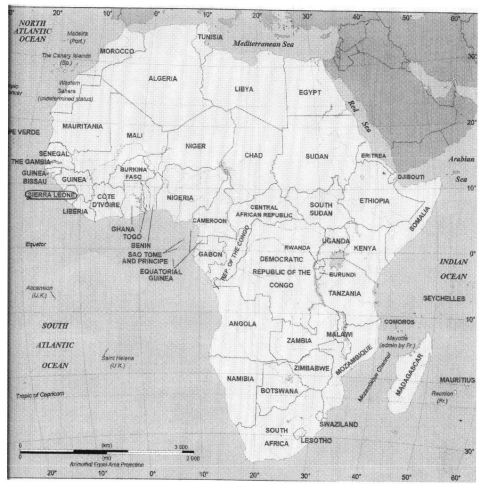

28. Map of the African continent 2011[42]

Wildlife in Sierra Leone include large game-animals such as elephants, lions, leopards, hyenas, and buffalo. Today many of these can only be found in national parks, but in the 1920s, they would have been in the wild and easily seen when walking from one village to another. There are also chimpanzees, monkeys, antelope, and bushpigs, along with hippopotamuses, crocodiles, and manatees. There are, of course, many, many insects, including the malaria-carrying mosquito and the tsetse fly.

While most histories of Sierra Leone begin in the 1700s with the resettlement of freed slaves in Freetown, archeological finds show that the country has been continuously inhabited for at least 2,500 years, and quite probably much longer. European explorers and traders began coming in the mid-1400s. Portuguese, Dutch, French, and English trading posts were established by the 1500s.

In 1787, the British helped 400 freed slaves from the United States, Nova Scotia, and Great Britain to return to Africa to settle in an area now known as Freetown, Sierra Leone. More displaced Africans were brought to Sierra Leone in the 1800s after the British abolished slave trade in 1807. It was also about this time that the British took over the administration of the colony and the British colonial governor of the region took up residency in Freetown. Although the British were able to make treaties with the indigenous chiefs in order to peacefully maintain their commerce interests, some of the traditional groups (notably the Temne and Mendi) felt that their freedom and culture were being threatened.[c]

In 1885, Britain decided that it needed to take more control over a larger territory, moving inland. By 1896, it declared Sierra Leone a "Protectorate" and put British citizens in charge of the government. To pay for the new administration, a heavy tax on dwellings was imposed. This led the indigenous chiefs to rebel and in February 1898, they started what became known as the Hut Tax War. Some resistance fighters staged an all-out attack on all foreign influences, killing whites and Africans associated with them. For a while, they held the advantage, but then the British governor ordered a "scorched earth policy" where the British burned entire villages,

---

[c] Most literature written during the colonial period of Sierra Leone history used terms such as "native," "tribe," or "native chief" to describe the indigenous people or groups. These terms today are understood to have negative connotations when describing Africans. Unless used in a direct quote, I have substituted more accurate and acceptable terminology such as "indigenous" or "local" people/rulers.

farmlands, and pastures. The war came to an end in November 1898, but not before more than 1,000 people were killed, including seven American United Brethren missionaries as well as many of the local missionaries. Additionally, almost all mission settlements were destroyed along with their records.

After this uprising, the British focused on maintaining law and order and set up new forms of government and reduced the power of the local chiefs. Sierra Leone continued to experience many turbulent times throughout much of the Twentieth Century. The country gained its independence in 1961.

Today, there are four principle divisions in the country: the Eastern, Northern, and Southern provinces, and the Western Area, sometimes called the Freetown Peninsula. These divisions are further divided into fourteen districts, and the districts are divided into 149 chiefdoms. There are many small villages within each chiefdom, some too small to be marked on most maps. For example, the Bumpe Chiefdom in which Rotifunk is located has 208 villages.[43]

In Freetown and some of the larger villages, many of the Sierra Leoneans could speak English. This was due, not only because of the British control of the country, but also because many of the freed slaves that were brought to Freetown knew the language. Additionally, British and American missionaries helped spread the use of the English language. Those who lived in the larger towns and villages also had access to education and were introduced to Western customs. In 1827, the Church Missionary Society (a British organization) founded Fourah Bay College to train African Christian leaders. This contributed to Freetown's reputation as the "Athens of West Africa." Fourah Bay College, was formerly affiliated with the University of Durham in the United Kingdom is today affiliated with the University of Sierra Leone.

Life for those who lived in the country's interior, where each local group had its own language and culture, was very different. They were mostly isolated and self-sufficient. They also lacked access to education and modern medicines to fight diseases such as cholera, typhoid, and malaria.

Some of the differences between the large city of Freetown and many of the villages can be seen in the photos below that are from postcards that Maud purchased. (The larger building in the photo of Westmoreland Street was the Law Courts building). Houses in Freetown were often cement with red corrugated iron roofs. In the villages, many of the houses were built of wood and mud and had a roof made of grass or bamboo, and hard-earth floors. They were usually one-story.

29. Street in Freetown, Sierra Leone, circa 1921

30. Village in Sierra Leone, circa 1921

The small houses in the villages were also often crowded with people of all ages. Most were relatives (close or distant) who lived there, but sometimes friends would come and stay indefinitely.[44] Women in these villages would work on the farm or in one of the arts and crafts businesses in town.

The arts and crafts of the indigenous people of Sierra Leone were numerous and included weaving, pottery, and basket-making. The woven cloths were known for their beauty and workmanship. Women would clean, spin and dye the cotton and then the men would weave and make up the cloth. Pottery was all made by hand without use of a potter's wheel. Baskets were made from various fibers, barks, and leaves and colored by using local vegetable dyes. They also made wooden furniture and wood and iron farm implements. Additionally, they created leather, gold, silver, ivory, and wooden decorative articles, along with ceremonial wooden masks.

31. Cloth weaving in Sierra Leone. Photo by Maud Hoyle

There are approximately seventeen ethnic groups in the country. Among them are the four groups that Maud primarily worked with: the Mende, Sherbro, Temne, and Kono. Each group has its own traditional religion. Most of these religions include belief in the existence of a supreme creator who is approached only by lesser gods, life after death, and a reliance on ancestors, spirits and the use of magic. Additionally, Islam was a fairly well-established religion in the area. When Maud was in Sierra Leone, there were still some indigenous groups that practiced cannibalism. The practices of polygamy and slavery were also prevalent at that time. Wealth was often counted, in part, by the number of wives a man had. Polygamy also played an important role economically as the wives did much of the labor on the farms. The more wives there were, the more work could be done. The missionaries preached strongly against polygamy and believed that no practicing polygamist should be a member of the church. However, the African preachers, understanding the arguments for polygamy, often softened the teaching by saying that monogamy was the preferred way to live, and they would still offer communion to any polygamist who wanted it.

The United Brethren in Sierra Leone[45]

Christian missionary work in Sierra Leone started in the early 17th Century. However, the efforts were sporadic due in part because the missionaries had difficulty adjusting to the climate and they also were affected by tropical diseases. Additionally, they faced resistance from those with strong beliefs in their own tribal religion or from those who had converted to Islam.

The United Brethren General Board of Missions sent their first missionaries to Sierra Leone in 1855. This effort failed as missionaries either died from tropical diseases or other ailments and conditions for which they could not be treated, or they chose to return home, unable to endure the hardships. Later, however, others went who were able to establish successful mission stations. In 1875, the United Brethren Women's Missionary Association decided to establish its own missions in the country. Working with the General Board, they chose Rotifunk as their first location. This was in a densely-populated territory up the Bompeh River that had no other Christian missionaries in the area. It is about fifty miles east of Freetown and the center of the Temne people. It was the first prominent city along the railroad to the interior and it became an important commercial and trading center. The Women's Association leased 100 acres for ninety-nine years and soon opened its mission station there. Between 1877 and 1898 (the year of the Hut Tax War), eighteen people, mostly unmarried women, served as United Brethren missionaries in Rotifunk.[46] This was a successful mission station, even after the killing of the missionaries during the war. Almost immediately, other missionaries volunteered to carry forward the work that the martyrs had begun.

Once the Rotifunk site was settled, the missionaries began taking extended trips into the interior of the country setting up preaching places and other mission stations. In all, the United Brethren established forty-four mission stations, with the headquarters in Freetown. The number of missionaries, pastors (always a local), teachers, and medical workers varied from site to site. In 1909 there were twelve foreign missionaries, twenty-eight African missionaries, ten churches, and 180 preaching places throughout the country. By 1929, the number had grown to twenty-five American missionaries, 100 Sierra Leoneans who ministered in 1,563 preaching places.[47]

In almost every station, the United Brethren set up separate boys and/or girls schools. Some were boarding schools and others were day schools. Many people believed that the primary purpose of mission schools was to teach students to read just well enough to read the Bible and, perhaps, a few other skills. However, most missionaries understood that it was important to teach practical knowledge and prepare students for employment after graduation. All students in the United Brethren schools, in addition to learning to read and write in their own language, also studied other academic subjects such as arithmetic, geography, grammar, psychology, science, and history. There were 2,146 students attending either the day or boarding schools in 1929.[48]

In terms of practical skills, the boys school such as the one that opened in Rotifunk in 1889 and the Albert Academy in Freetown (established in 1904), taught students to make bricks, cement, and furniture and how to grow pineapple, bananas, coffee, rice, and yams. The boys would work several hours a day putting these skills into practice in exchange for room and board.

32. Schoolhouse in Rotifunk. Photo taken by Maud Hoyle

In the early years, girls were taught to become Christian homemakers and not to rely on primitive or superstitious beliefs. They would learn to cook, sew, and keep house, in addition to nursing and caring for children, incorporating Western standards of hygiene, nutrition, and health. Today it is recognized that the education of women was one of the most positive contributions of Protestant missions.[49] Perhaps, most important, it protected them from early, childhood marriages.[50] Tying the curriculum together in all the schools was the predominant teaching about the love of God.

The boys and girls, ranging in age from four to twenty, would come from many miles away, some on train; others by foot. Each would be given a bed with a grass-filled mattress. For some who were from remote villages, this was the first bed that they had ever slept on.[51]

Extending their commitment to education, the missionaries also started the first Bumpe Chiefdom Library in Rotifunk in November 1926.[52] The 243 volumes were available to all people in the chiefdom.

Today the United Methodist Church in Sierra Leone operates 213 elementary and twenty secondary schools, many of which were started by the United Brethren. These include the Harford School for Girls in Moyamba which opened in 1900 and the Albert Academy for Boys in Freetown.

As was stated earlier, the United Brethren strongly believed that it was not enough to be concerned with the spiritual needs of the people by sharing only the words of the Gospel. It was equally important to show God's love through action and to help improve their physical and socio-economic conditions. Providing education to the local Africans was one way. Another was to provide them with medical care. The first medical missionary in Sierra Leone was Dr. Marietta Hatfield, who arrived in Rotifunk in 1891. She was later assisted by Dr. Mary Archer. These two physicians were killed during the Hut Tax War and later the hospital there was named after them.

By 1929, the United Brethren operated five hospitals and dispensaries in Sierra Leone. However, often these were run by only a single nurse as there were not enough physicians in the field. The medical personnel had to be competent in treating patients from head to toe. At times, they needed to serve as physician, optometrist, dentist, or surgeon. Following the example of Jesus, the doctors and nurses treated men, women, and children alike. For the missionaries, this was yet another way of demonstrating that God cared for each individual, male or female, adult or child. Many Africans were astonished at this level of benevolence.[53]

While the Africans were deeply aware and appreciative of the missionaries' concern for their health, education, and souls, they also felt pain caused by the feeling of superiority that many of the missionaries had. As John and Rena Karefa-Smart explain in their book, *The Halting Kingdom*, this was the colonists' and missionaries' "blackest mark."[54] Generally speaking, missionaries in the early years had little understanding or knowledge about the African people and their customs. Their mission stations were patterned after the life the missionary was accustomed to in his/her own country. Little, if any, attempt was made to incorporate indigenous music, art, or other forms of worship into the Christian churches.[55]

Fortunately, by the end of World War I, this attitude began to change. For example, the United Brethren Board of Missions began specifically instructing missionary candidates that they must work with the African pastors as brothers who are equal. An illustration of this was found in a 1929 letter which the General Secretary of the Board of Missions wrote to a newly appointed missionary. The General Secretary wrote,

> You must remember that you are going to black people who have for a long time been considered by average Americans as an inferior race. Any evidence of race superiority or race prejudice will immediately defeat the influence and usefulness of any missionary. I am aware that most of us are conscious of the spirit of race discrimination within our souls. We must all fight against it.[56]

Preparing for the Journey[d]

Having done her research, Maud was then ready to prepare for her new life. The 1894 *Manual* included a more detailed list of items missionaries should take to Africa. Included were "an old dress for ocean travel," four cotton and eight gingham dresses, two pairs high shoes and four pairs low walking shoes (all a size larger than worn at home), one white dress hat and two plain broad-rim hats, two dozen cakes of soap, a pair of dress gloves as needed when in New York, safety pins, pencils, pens (but no ink), and writing paper, books, and "little things you should want to make your room cozy, convenient, or comfortable."[57] This might include pillows,

---

[d] Much of the details about preparation for the trip, the voyage, and descriptions of Sierra Leone have been taken from the diaries and letters of Lloyd Mignerey, another United Brethren missionary who served in Sierra Leone from 1922–1924. His first assignment was at Rotifunk where Maud was also working. References from specific letters are listed in the Endnotes.

books, pictures, musical instruments, materials for sewing and knitting, and possibly hard candy.

It was also recommended that missionaries going to a tropical location take a medical kit which would include medicines to control diarrhea, constipation, and pain, along with large amounts of quinine for malaria prevention. They were instructed to take one tablet of quinine, three to four times every day.

A crucial step in preparing for the journey was to apply for a passport and for a British Permit to enter British dominions. The Board of Missions would pay for the passport and for the cost of the trip to the mission site. At the time that Maud applied for her passport, three references were required. The passport, permit, and letters of reference needed to be endorsed in person at the British Consul in New York City forty-eight hours prior to sailing. Maud began this process by applying for her passport on September 23, 1920.

As noted in the application, Maud planned to leave New York on November 20, but that was not to be. In a letter from the Foreign Missionary Society headquarters dated October 1920, the General Secretary noted that her trip had been delayed, explaining that

> When her appointment was made we asked her to write to the persons whose names she had given as reference. This she did, but after waiting about two months, we received word from the British Passport Office that one of the men to whom a letter had been sent had not replied. Upon inquiry it was learned that he had misplaced it. Because of the delay the passport Bureau sent him a second letter, and he had not returned that. When Miss Hoyle made a second inquiry at our suggestion, she found that he had not sent an answer to the second letter, so Miss Hoyle then sent another reference. But this is all taking precious time. We have asked the Passport Bureau if they will not cable at our expense. I do not know what they may see fit to do. It is unnecessary to say that I regret this delay very much.[58]

33. Maud's Passport and Travel Papers

Apparently, the Passport Bureau did not expedite the process and/or there were other reasons that caused a much longer delay in Maud leaving. It wasn't until sometime in June 1921 that Maud sailed to Sierra Leone.

In the meantime, Rev. James Replogle, Maud's former pastor at the Lagonda Avenue Church in Springfield, wrote an introduction of Maud to the missionary world which appeared in the January 1921 issue of *The Evangel.*

> It is a delight to write of a friend, especially one whose life has been dedicated to the service of Christ. When but an infant, Miss Hoyle was taken seriously ill. When her life was despaired of, her mother kneeled by her side and promised God, if He would restore her to health, she would dedicate her to him. Her mother today is paying her vow as she makes the supreme sacrifice in sending her daughter to Africa.
>
> Miss Hoyle was reared in a Christian home, one in which the fires were kept burning on the family altar. Her education has been largely obtained through her own earnest, patient, and persistent efforts. While her pastor, I often heard her express her desire to take up some special Christian work….
>
> Miss Hoyle is appreciated in her home church because of her continued and faithful activity as a member of that church. She is serious, devout, studious, a hard worker, and a most earnest and consistent Christian. I believe she is eminently prepared for the work she is soon to take up, and know she goes to her new task after much thought and prayer, and believe she will be happy and successful in her work for Christ in Africa.[59]

Following this introduction was Maud's response:

> Since my conversion, I have longed to be a coworker in the advancement of Christ's kingdom here. While in the Seminary, I became a Volunteer. Although I had entered into Christian service, the great need of the benighted lands continued to call me. I could not give up, so continued to make full preparation. When the word of my appointment to Rotifunk, Sierra Leone, West Africa, came, I was filled with great joy, and now, as I go, I have the assurance that God is guiding and that He will protect. I have made a full surrender to Him. I believe my commission is directly from God, and I want to keep so close to Him that I will not hesitate to do what He places in my hand. Will you kindly remember me in your prayers; also, my mother, as she will be quite lonely after my departure.[60]

Before Maud left, the Columbus Avenue church held a consecration service for her. This service, outlined by the Women's Missionary Association,[61] allowed missionary candidates to give remarks and to state that they felt called by God to missionary work and to publicly consecrate themselves to God and to the work they were about to undertake. The service would end with a prayer asking for God's blessing on the missionary as they started on their journey. With this support and her strong faith, Maud left for Africa.

Making the Trip

Maud traveled from Springfield to New York City by train, probably in late May or early June 1921. It is doubtful that Maud had ever been in New York before and she must have marveled at all the sights and sounds. While there, she took care of routine business such as securing steamer tickets, having her passport authorized, and possibly purchasing special tropical supplies unavailable in Ohio.[62] It is likely that she would have spent several days in the city.

The exact date that Maud left the port at New York to sail to England is not known. However, there is a photo that she took of New York as the ship pulled out.

34. Ship leaving New York harbor. Photo by Maud Hoyle.

What excitement she must have felt being on the ocean and seeing its vastness for the first time! It generally took ten days to get from New York to Liverpool. During that time, there were undoubtedly some rough spots at sea. While we will never know if Maud ever experienced seasickness, it was a frequent ailment of first time voyagers.

Meal times on the ship were typically 8:30 a.m. for breakfast, 1:00 for lunch, 4:00 for tea, with dinner at 8:30 p.m. It was probable that Maud shared her meals with missionaries from other denominations heading toward stations in other parts of Africa.

Once she arrived in Liverpool, she again experienced exhilaration—this time of being in a new country with its unique customs. She would have checked in with the United Brethren Headquarters in Liverpool and probably spent some time at the School of Tropical Medicine. This school was founded in 1898 and was the first institution in the world dedicated to research and teaching in the field of tropical medicine. Maud may have purchased additional tropical supplies such as mosquito netting, a pith helmet, sun umbrella, and more quinine ("the great remedy of the tropics"). Some missionaries, if they had enough time in England, went to London and toured the historical sites. It is doubtful, though, that Maud would have had the money to do this.

Maud left Liverpool on June 22, 1921, to complete her journey to Sierra Leone, sailing on the *Zaria*.[63] On the following page is a picture she took of the wharf at Liverpool as the ship pulled out.

The voyage from Liverpool to Freetown, Sierra Leone took anywhere between nine to twelve days, with three stops along the way at the Madeira Islands, followed by the Canary Islands, and then Conakry (which today is the capital of Guinea).[64] Finally, looking through her porthole, Maud got her first glimpse of the country in which she would spend much of the next ten years.

35. Wharf at Liverpool. Photo by Maud Hoyle.

Once the ship was anchored, she boarded a rowboat that took her to shore. She must have felt such excitement as she stepped out of the boat and onto land. Here, in Sierra Leone, she could now begin fulfilling her life's dream and calling.

Chapter Seven:
How Beautiful Are the Feet

And how can anyone preach unless they are sent? As it is written:
"How beautiful are the feet of those who bring good news!"
— Romans 10:15 (NIV)

Rotifunk

After spending several days in Freetown at the United Brethren mission house, where she rested from the voyage and learned more about her new country, Maud boarded a train to Rotifunk. Because the train only ran at about ten to twelve miles per hour and made many stops along the way, the trip took over four hours to go fifty-five miles. Looking out the window of the train car, Maud saw long stretches of brush, palm, banana, and mango trees, along with fields of rice and peanuts.

When the train arrived in Rotifunk, Maud was welcomed by one of the missionaries from the compound. Although we do not have verification of this, it is likely that the missionary was Etta Odle, Maud's former classmate from Bonebrake, who had been serving in Sierra Leone since 1910. Over the years, Miss Odle had sent Maud a few postcards expressing her hope that Maud would serve in Sierra Leone. Now, with Maud's arrival, her prayers had been answered.

Some of the boys from the school also came to the train station and they carried Maud's boxes and luggage on their heads as they walked to the mission house as shown in the picture following which Maud took.

36. Locals carrying trunks on head. Photo by Maud Hoyle.

During the half-mile walk from the train station to the mission, Maud took in all the sights, sounds, and smells of her new village. Rotifunk had about one hundred houses and it was a commercial center because of the crossing of the Bompeh River with the railway line to Freetown. As such, there was a mingling of people and languages from various indigenous groups, including the Sherbro, Mendi, Temne, Lokko, and Susu.

As she walked by the houses, Maud noticed that most had low mud walls with few or no windows and long slanting roofs. She also saw the children playing in the streets. Many of them wore only a necklace of large black and red beads or nothing at all. She noticed that even most of the adults wore the minimum of clothing—usually nothing more than a cloth about the waist. However, there were some who wore the long flowing gowns common to Eastern countries. Almost everyone was barefoot. Her friend Etta would have told her about the town market where rice, couscous, fish, peanuts, and fresh produce were sold daily, with beef being available only once a week.[65] As she walked closer to the mission station, she also spotted its farm, which

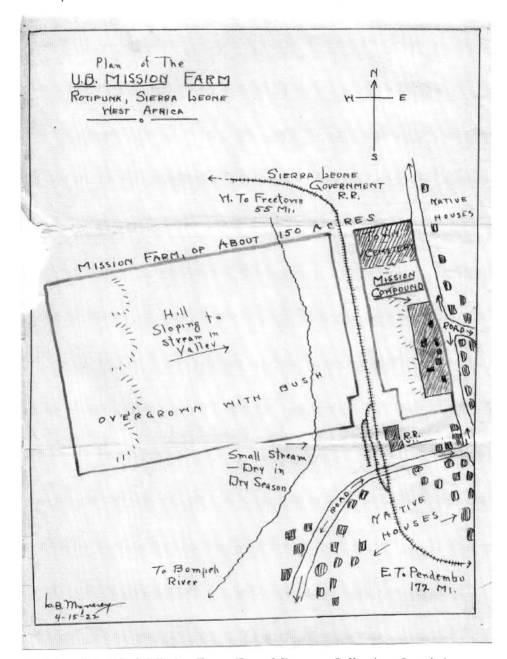

37. Map of Rotifunk Mission Farm. From Mignerey Collection, Otterbein University Archives.

had coconut, banana, and mango trees, along with many pineapple plants.

At long last, Maud took her first steps onto the mission grounds, entering from the south and past the mission cemetery. She paused there to remember the five missionaries who were murdered while the entire mission compound was destroyed during the Hut Tax War. Up ahead, she gazed at all the mission buildings. First, there was the school, and then the mission house, and church. She marveled at the brave and determined foreign and local workers who rebuilt this entire mission after the war and remembered that the Martyrs Memorial Church had been mostly paid for and built by the local Sierra Leoneans.

38. Martyrs Memorial Church, Rotifunk, Sierra Leone. Photo by Maud Hoyle.

Just past the church was the dispensary where Maud would spend most of her time while stationed there. Beyond that was the local pastor's home, a house of mud and sticks roofed with tin. Behind the dispensary was the Mission Boy's home, a large two-story wooden building. An open shed near the home served as a kitchen where the boys did their own cooking.

Although Maud was physically exhausted from her journey, before going to the mission house to settle in, she first stopped at the church to thank God for her safe journey and to pray for strength and wisdom as she began her new work.

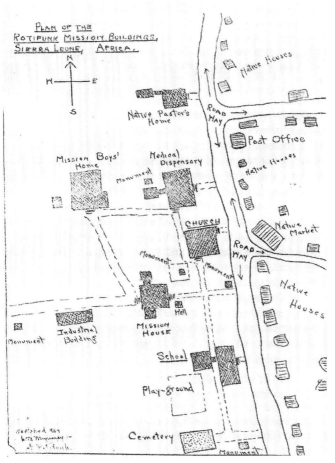

39. Rotifunk Mission Compound, Sketch by Lloyd Mignerey. Photo from Jeremy H. Smith's *Staircase of a Patron*, p.91.

As Maud approached the mission house, she saw three steps leading to the entrance of the two-story, 950 square-feet dwelling.[66] When she entered, she found that the first story was more of an above ground basement. The missionaries lived on the second story which was surrounded by a covered porch with the south side and half the east front of the porch being screened. Maud was given a brief tour of the five rooms and the kitchen, which was 20' x 12'. There was also an attic with two rooms. The cook used one of them for her living room. It was the only house on mission field that had screened windows and doors. A tin roof covered the entire house.

Maud's room, located on the backside of the house, was simply furnished, as was the entire house. The United Brethren Missionary Association furnished everything except curtains and bed linens. Her bed came equipped with a net over it to provide additional protection from mosquitoes and other flying bugs and beetles that swarmed through the night air. Candles and kerosene lamps provided light throughout the house at night.

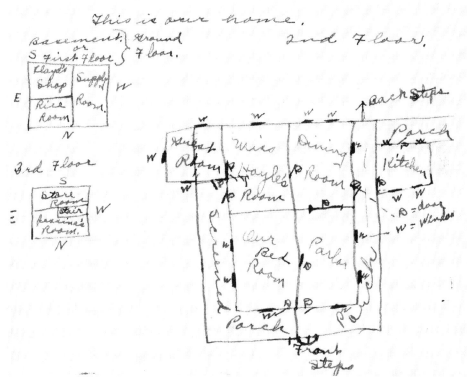

40. Diagram of the mission house. Note the location of "Miss Hoyle's room." From Mignerey Collection, Otterbein University Archives.

Maud learned that a local cook prepared the meals and did the laundry for the missionaries. Meals almost always included rice, along with fish or meat, and fresh vegetables and fruits. The missionaries generally liked the traditional African food, but they would also import some food such as dry cereals, tea, and canned milk. Mealtime was also the usual time to take their daily doses of quinine.

Because of the extreme heat and humidity, the missionaries changed their clothes often. The local women washed the clothes in the river by pounding them on a stone until clean. Then, to iron the clothes, the cloth was placed across a thick, heavy wooden slab and beaten with a heavy smooth rounded wooden club about 15" long, until pounded smooth.

41. Women washing clothes in river.

The humidity also caused the ever-present mold on everything—clothes, shoes, books, the furniture, and walls and floors. Small red ants would invade the house "by the millions," and spiders, roaches, and grasshoppers, all described as "enormous," also made their ways into the house.

Life in Africa was definitely a big adjustment for Maud, but her faith was strong, and she knew that God was with her always. She was eager and ready to get to work!

Rotifunk Dispensary

Maud's first assignment in Sierra Leone was to serve as the nurse and run the dispensary at Rotifunk. She worked there as a temporary replacement for Nora Vesper, who was on furlough until September 1922. "Miss Vesper," as she was always called, was one of the most dedicated missionaries in Sierra Leone, serving in Rotifunk from 1915–1955. During the years that Maud was in Africa, she often filled in for Miss Vesper whenever she took her furloughs.

The dispensary was established in 1901 in the basement of the mission home. Five years later, the new Hatfield-Archer Dispensary opened, named after the two doctors who were killed in the Hut Tax War. This facility was a one and a half story building, 45' x 22' with a corrugated iron roof and a wide veranda all around it. It was in this building that Maud began her work in Africa.[e]

The Dispensary in Rotifunk

42. Dispensary in Rotifunk. Photo from *The Evangel.* Vol. XLIX, No. 6, 1930: 174.

---

[e] During the 1992–2002 civil war in Sierra Leone, the United Methodist Hatfield Archer Memorial Hospital was burned down. "Most of the staff fled and the hospital's charred and empty shell was used as a primitive clinic." Thanks to the United Methodist Church in Norway, the hospital was completely renovated and reopened on May 24, 2014. (Frisbie, Julia. "Rotifunk Hospital Re-Opens." United Methodist Committee on Relief. News Archives. June 19, 2014. http://www.umcor.org/UMCOR/Resources/News-Stories/2014/June/0619rotifunk.)

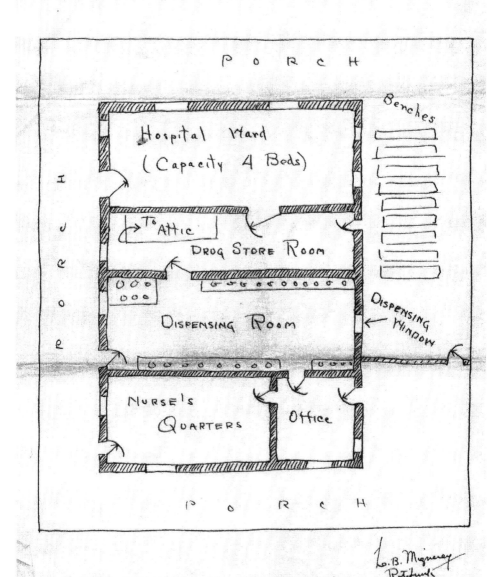

43. Hatfield-Archer Dispensary, Rotifunk, Sierra Leone. Drawing by Lloyd Mignerey, September 27, 1922. Mignerey Collection, Otterbein University Archives

News about the dispensary and medical care spread quickly after it opened. It was considered to be the best equipped in the country outside of Freetown. Many people came from long distances, some traveling as many as twelve days on foot to reach the mission for treatment. The number of cases treated each year increased from about 200 when it first opened to over 5,000 in 1921, and more than 10,000 in 1929.

As a medical missionary, Maud wanted to heal people physically and spiritually. She was able to do this, in part, by following a practice started by Miss Vesper at the Rotifunk Dispensary. The dispensary sold medicine on Monday, Wednesday, and Friday mornings. But before any medicine was dispersed, the patients were required to sit on the benches on the front porch while the nurse or a local staff person proclaimed the gospel story. These mini-sermons were given in Mende or Temne, or both if necessary.[67] For Maud to continue this practice, she had to learn to speak both languages.

Generally, the United Brethren Church encouraged missionaries to spend much of their first three months learning the local language(s). However, Maud did not have that luxury; she had to learn them quickly while on the job. She was fortunate that many of the people who lived in Rotifunk spoke English or Krio (Creole)[f], and they could translate for her when needed.

Of course, Maud's primary job was to treat patients who came to the clinic with one of a countless number of possible ailments. These could range from leprosy to venereal diseases to infected teeth. Because of the extreme shortage of doctors in the field, Maud, like most nurses, had to diagnose diseases, prescribe medicines, perform some surgeries, and extract teeth.

---

[f] In colonial parlance, many African languages are routinely called dialects. However, Creole, now spelled Krio, is the name of the formerly enslaved people and returnees who settled the Freetown peninsula. Krio is also the name of a language that evolved from local and other African (especially Yoruba) and European (Portuguese, French, and English) languages.

One of the strangest childhood illnesses that Maud dealt with was caused by eating dirt. This habit would begin when children ate rice that they had accidentally dropped to the ground. When they scooped up the rice, they also picked up some dirt. They then would acquire a peculiar taste for dirt and later lick the mud walls of their houses. The dirt caused the entire body to swell and often led to death.[68] Other illnesses were caused by people drinking water from the same streams in which they bathed and washed their clothes.[69]

Mignerey described one of Maud's cases where a little boy had been brought in with a lower lip that had become badly infected from a cut made three weeks earlier. The lip had begun to decompose and an open, running sore three inches in diameter was spreading over the child's cheek. Maud decided that the only way to save the child was to operate. Mignerey gave the chloroform and Pastor Smart, the local pastor, assisted Maud "in drawing the pieces of the lip together and sewing them in place. We then placed a wet dressing held in place by adhesives above the head, over the immense sore."[70]

In another letter, Mignerey told of a second time when he again assisted Maud in surgery. The patient had been run over by a train as he had tried to hop on. Mignerey gave the chloroform while Maud "probed, cleaned, sewed, and bound the feet." Later, the patient was transferred to the hospital in Freetown.[71]

Other Duties, as Assigned

In addition to her nursing and dispensary responsibilities, Maud had other duties. One was particularly unexpected. Two years before Maud got there, Miss Vesper had taken in a three-day old infant when her mother had died. When Vesper went on furlough, Maud was responsible for caring for the child who was named Ellen. According to a letter that Mrs. Mignerey wrote,

44. In front of the Mission House: Yanco(?) Betty Smart, Ellen. Photo taken by Maud Hoyle.

Ellen was quite a handful but well loved.[72] Among Maud's artifacts is a letter that Ellen wrote to Maud dated February 29, 1958. Ellen addressed the letter to "My dear Aunty Hoyle" and signed it "Your child Ellen." In the letter, Ellen told Maud that she was working as a matron on the Jiama EUB Mission Girls Home and that she heard often from "Ma Vesper."

There was another child that held a special place in Maud's heart and that was the local pastor's daughter. The United Brethren mission stations always had a local pastor who oversaw all church activities. In Rotifunk, the minister was James Alfred Karefa-Smart, and he

45. Workers at Rotifunk, from left: Mr. Labourne (teacher), Mr. Williams (teacher), Rev. Smart (pastor), Nora Vesper (missionary in charge of station), Vera Rettew (teacher), Mrs. Smart (pastor's wife), Maud Hoyle (nurse) holding Maude Smart (pastor's baby).

was considered one of the best pastors in the country.[73] Pastor Smart worked closely with all the missionaries, but he must have thought most highly of Maud, as he named one of his children after her. Maud kept dozens of photos from her time in Sierra Leone. However, the photo on the previous page showing her holding her namesake is the only photo in her collection in which she herself appears.

Here are two more photos of Maude Smart. The first shows Maude on the left with her friend Nora Caulker. The second one shows Maude feeding a baby leopard.

46. Maude Smart and Nora Caulker

47. Maude Smart feeding baby leopard

Another major obligation for all missionaries was, of course, to proclaim the Gospel. All missionaries and missionary wives taught Sunday school or led prayer meetings held throughout the week. But their main "preaching job" was to travel to small villages to preach.

This practice was called "itinerating." Again, we do not have details of Maud's own experiences in this endeavor, but we do have descriptions from other missionaries. When itinerating, the missionaries and a group of converts walked several miles or went by boat, reaching as many as forty villages in a day to preach the message of salvation. This was demanding work, sometimes requiring them to walk five or six miles in the sun (or heavy rainstorms during the rainy season). It was common to have to wade through swamps or rivers.[74] Many villages consisted of just three or four houses tucked away in the bush within a two hour walk of Rotifunk, although the missionaries generally focused on the larger villages of thirty-five to fifty homes.

In one of Mignerey's letters, he described an approach that he took when itinerating. When arriving at a village, he often asked the chief for use of his front porch to hold a service. Then he went about the village inviting all the people to attend. The service began with songs sung in the local Temne language which attracted more people to attend. This was followed by a prayer in Temne. Mignerey preached in English, but had an interpreter. In trying to relate the stories of the Bible in ways that the Africans could understand, he used "rice" instead of "bread" and "fish" instead of meat. The primary message was always to teach that God is a God of love who heals, forgives, and provides. Conversion was always voluntary and never coerced.[75]

Susan Bachman, another missionary in Sierra Leone, described itinerating as joyful work. "The people love to have you squat down with them and hold the baby, try to spin the cotton, scrape the ginger or whatever work it is that they are doing."[76] It was another way of making Christ known and loved. While there are no accounts of Maud's own experience itinerating, it is certain that she, too, found joy in sharing God's love when she met the people wherever they were.

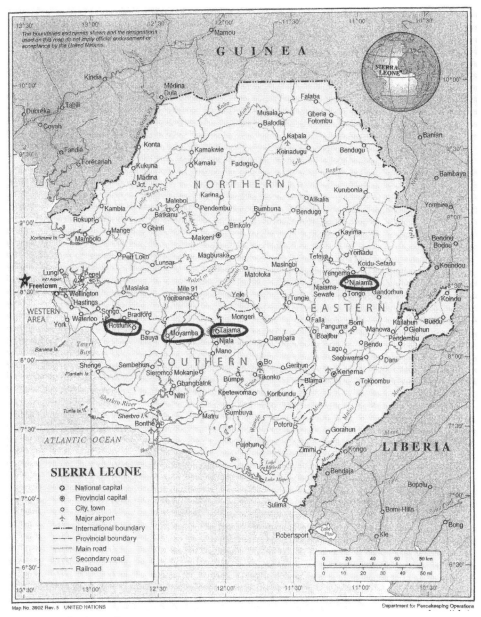

48. Map of Sierra Leone

Stepping Out

As noted earlier, Maud's appointment in Rotifunk was only temporary until Miss Vesper returned from furlough sometime in mid-1922. Maud was then sent to Moyamba. This was the first of several transfers that Maud would experience during the next eight years. She would also spend time in Taiama and Jiama (Njiama), with a few junkets off and on in Rotifunk.

The Moyamba mission began in 1899 and was located twenty-one miles east of Rotifunk. It was the chief center of the Mendi people and had a large English-speaking population. This was one of the larger United Brethren sites in Sierra Leone and had twelve workers. The mission station had a church, a three-room school, houses for the local teachers and the missionaries, and the Harford School for Girls.

While in Moyamba, Maud was responsible for the dispensary and taking care of all the medical needs of those in the mission station and the local villages. The Board of Missions reported that "during a serious typhoid epidemic [in Moyamba], she nursed many of the girls back to health."[77] In the afternoons, she taught in the Lillian R. Harford School for Girls, which was a new experience for her. In a letter that Maud wrote to Mrs. Mignerey (who was still in Rotifunk), she said

> I never thought I would write to you from Moyamba. Well here I am for one year. My work here is quite different as you know.... I have a class of twenty little girls. They do quite nicely. They are sewing on paper now. They know how to back stitch and button hole stitch. Tomorrow I am going to give them cross stitch. I think maybe next week they will start on quilt blocks. I never thought I would be called to teach, but one ever knows. I may be called on yet to cook. Oh, my, I pity those who will have to put up with it if I do.[78]

49. Sewing class in Moyamba. Photo by Maud Hoyle.

It appears that Maud was willing and able to accept whatever duties she was assigned, knowing that in everything, she was serving her God.

Maud must have done a good job teaching the girls to sew. An article in *The Evangel* mentioned that there was an exhibit held during commencement celebrations that included sewing, crocheting, and embroidering work, along with picture frames made from hammered brass, baked bread, and soap made at the school.

> The showing made by the graduates and students in the exercises of this commencement is a good indication of the high standard of industrial and literary work maintained in this school through the efforts of Miss Naomi Wilson, the matron, Miss Lela Gipson, Miss Maud Hoyle, of the missionary staff, and the native teachers and assistants.[79]

In Maud's 1923 Annual Report (which covered July 1922–June 1923), she mentioned that she preached about once a month at the church in Moyamba. She also was in charge of the Women's Association there. This must have presented some challenges as she wrote "Those who know anything about these organizations need ask no questions."[80] One can only surmise what those challenges were. She also reported that she relieved Miss Vesper at the Dispensary in Rotifunk for three weeks in February. Upon returning to Moyamba she

> ...had just gotten settled again when a telegram from Taiama came saying 'Come, hammock will be at Mano.' So I packed my few belongings and in two hours was on my way. Arriving at our mission in Taiama I found Miss Eaton quite sick. In a few weeks Miss Eaton was much improved but the work being too heavy for one missionary I was asked to remain for the remainder of the year.[81]

The United Brethren established its Taiama mission in 1896, but it was destroyed two years later by the English during the war. It reopened in 1901 and the branch dispensary opened in 1908. Most of the time, there were eight workers. Taiama is located about fifty miles northeast of Moyamba. In Taiama, Maud had charge of the dispensary, a class of seventeen boys in industrial work in the mornings, and another class of thirty boys in the afternoon.

Maud certainly experienced many adventures while in Africa. One family story that her great-nephew John Hoyle remembers hearing involved a large snake and a young child. Maud heard a child screaming and as she entered the room to comfort him, she spotted a large snake curled around the bannister. Maud walked outside and picked up a piece of a very dense wood that they called "iron wood" and went back inside and clubbed the snake to death. She seemed fearless, but she certainly would tell others that she just did what needed to be done and trusted that the Lord would keep her safe.

While in Taiama, it was common for Maud to see 200 patients a day with almost half needing injections for yaws, a chronic, disfiguring infectious disease affecting the bones, joints, and skin. Maud summarized her other work here in her 1923 annual report by writing,

> ...I believe it would be easier to tell what I have not done than to tell what I have done. But as a summary I will say that I have filled the office this year of a surgeon, physician, nurse, optometrist, teacher, preacher, itinerant, anesthetist, dentist, dress-maker, and tailor. The year has been full of change but an eye-opener to me pertaining to mission work. I have enjoyed the year and only wish it were possible to remain longer.[82]

Maud wasn't able to remain longer in Taiama because it was time for her to go home on furlough.

Furlough

Because the work of missionaries, particularly those serving in the tropics, was strenuous, the United Brethren Board of Missions insisted that they take occasional breaks from their work. For a short retreat, missionaries in Sierra Leone could go to Bethany Cottage, a "rest cottage" with eight rooms located on Mt.

84 | BEAUTIFUL FEET

Leicester, which was just south of Freetown. The cottage was located on two acres of ground which sat 1550 feet above sea level. Here, the temperature was cooler and there were fewer mosquitos. Missionaries could spend four to six weeks resting here during the years between their furloughs.

However, the Board of Missions recognized that short vacations were not enough of a break to become fully rested and they gave the missionaries orders to return home after every two years of service (this was later changed to every three years). Furloughs generally lasted eleven months. This enabled the missionaries "to restore the exhausted energies of those laboring in trying climates and to stimulate the Church at home by bringing it into touch with the laborers abroad."[83] The Board paid for the travel expenses home and additionally gave an allowance of $62.50 per month for unmarried missionaries and $115 for each married couple during the furlough. Salaries for missionaries while in the field varied from location and were based on the local cost of living. The salary was sufficient "with wise economy, for comfortable support; 'not sufficient to compensate for defects in financial management'...."[84]

Maud left Sierra Leone for her first furlough sometime in July 1923. After a brief layover in England, she sailed on the *Belegenland* and arrived in New York on August 4.[85]

From there, she went to Maryland for two months where she spoke at various churches. One of her joys was to spend time with her grandparents, Joseph and Charlotte Hoyle. This would be the last time she would see them as they died before she could return there again. Maud also spent several days speaking at the United Brethren Church in Latrobe, Pennsylvania before going to Ohio. Here she spoke at many churches of all denominations. She also assisted in a two-week revival meeting in Strasburg, Ohio.[86] This was one of the churches which supported her financially. At this revival, the topics of her sermons were "Lost Sheep Sought and Found," "Occasions of Hope for Salvation That Have Not Availed," "Long Walk for Young Converts," and "The Supremacy of Christ."[87] She, of course, also spoke at the Columbus Avenue Church in Springfield.

Before leaving home to go back to Africa, Maud had another complete physical as required by the Mission Board. She also wrote a letter about her time on furlough for *The Evangel* where she ended it once again asking for prayers for herself and for her mother: "Now, will you, as I leave again, please pray for mother as well as for the work and workers? I believe that you did this during my last term, and oh, how it helped!"[88]

Maud's niece, Dorothy Hoyle Cash, remembered being at the train station when Maud left to go back to Africa in the summer of 1924. Dorothy was three-years-old at the time and she wore a dress that had a very large hem. She recalled thinking that the hem could be let out as she grew, and she could wear it the next time her Aunt Maud would be home, making it easier for Maud to recognize her!

50. Dress Dorothy Hoyle wore to see Maud off at train station, 1924. Picture taken by Faith Schiffer.

Pressing Onward in Africa

Maud spent much of the next two years working in Rotifunk, Taiama, and Moyamba. The best way to understand her work is through her own words. Below is an article that Maud wrote which appeared in the October 1925 issue of *The Evangel* and describes just one day of her work.

> As I sit with pen in hand tonight after a busy day in the dispensary, trying to jot down in a few words something about our medical work here, the words of Jesus come to me: "They that are whole need not a physician: but they that are sick." "I came not to call the righteous but sinners to repentance."
>
> During the past few days, we have had all types of people as well as diseases to cope with.
>
> Here comes a man with a downcast look. He is full of leprosy, a mass of corruption, dying bit by bit. Following him is a child of about one year of age. The little hand is ready to drop off from the wrist. From a sore in the thigh you can see up into the abdomen. The mouth is so sore it can hardly swallow, yet it tries to nurse from the mother's breast, which is so swollen from elephantiasis it hangs into her lap."
>
> Then come a number so large that you at home would not believe it possible, with the most loathsome venereal diseases. The patients are just as badly off as those who have leprosy—noses off, fingers off, ulcers over the body, limbs, and arms so large and deep, with such a stench, it is unpleasant to go near them.
>
> Then comes a young girl, quite beautiful, though wasting away by the dread disease of tuberculosis. Her people claim she is a witch, so they will not take proper care of her, for the sooner she dies the better.
>
> Some of our boys come for the stretcher. There is a man quite ill to be brought from the incoming train. They will not take him farther, as they claim he is dying. He is placed in the ward with a little boy who was badly burned the evening before. We give him a hypodermic of Ementine, ask God's blessing upon him, and try to forget long enough to partake of a little food at noon-time. While trying to relax a little, the voices are heard again, "Please, ma." Sometimes not much is wanted—only a little iodoform powder or a dose of salts. Again, it is apt to be an accident case. Just today I sent a man to Freetown who had fallen from a tree and sustained a compound fracture of the right wrist. His body was covered with sores and scars. With the assistance of Reverend Smart, I replaced the bone and put the wrist in splints.
>
> The need for medical work is great, and affords such a wonderful opportunity to present to the patients the Great Healer of the soul. If we were only privileged to have a doctor in this needy field!

I will just mention how these cases are met. First with prayer. I would not dare to undertake the treatment of any kind of case without first turning to the Great Physician and asking His help. If the people were spiritually and morally healthy, many more would have healthy bodies.

In the second place, we gain their confidence and in this way, decide upon what treatment they require.

As we meet these cases day after day among all types of people, some eager and willing to hear the Word, other obstinate and impatient, we have cause at times for rejoicing; then at other times we do not dare to think, only trust, knowing if we continue to do His will the people will someday know Him, believe in Him, and surrender their lives to Him. For this we pray and labor day by day. Will you join with us in this great task?[89]

Clearly, Maud had a formidable task in caring for all these people. It is also clear that she continued to walk with God with complete trust and assurance.

Letters to the home Mission Board office written by missionaries in charge of various stations in Sierra Leone would often include discussions of problems with some missionaries. Some were often ill; some were ill-tempered and caused discontent. The only issue ever mentioned about Maud was that she was sometimes late in turning in her annual report. After reading her accounting of a single day's work and of her devotion to caring for her patients, no one considered this to be a problem.

Maud left for her second furlough in June 1926. She was able to sail directly to New York from Freetown, leaving on June 28 on the *Cathlamet*, and arriving in New York on July 16.[90]

While we do not have as much information about what she did during this furlough, we do know that she spoke several times at the Fall Institute of the Miami (Ohio) Conference of the Women's Missionary Association[91] and preached at the Hyde Park United Brethren Church in Cincinnati.[92] Also, while home, Maud renewed her passport in the spring of 1927.

51. Passport, issued March 28, 1927.

However, she apparently did much more while in the United States. The General Secretary of the United Brethren Board of Missions wrote a letter to Maud in May 1927, shortly before she boarded the ship in New York to return to Africa. In it he stated,

> I hope that the furlough has given you time for rest and recuperation such as one needs after a term of service in the tropics. I followed with much interest your itinerary and felt a number of times that perhaps you were doing too much..., but I know how tremendous the pressure is and how anxious churches and pastors are to have a missionary visit their church.[93]

Before leaving for Africa, this time for a three-year term, Maud once again requested *The Evangel* readers "to please remember mother in your prayers, that God will watch over and protect her, and that she may at all times have sweet communion with Him we all love and serve...."[94]

For this third tour of duty, Maud was assigned to Jiama located in the Kono district. This remote mission station was located two hundred miles from the ocean and sixty miles from the nearest railway station. It had been established in 1910 and had a branch dispensary and hospital.

52. Hospital in Jiama. Photo by Maud Hoyle.

53. School boys in Jiama. Photo by Maud Hoyle.

Another of the family stories told of a time when Maud was going through "bush country" with her guide and luggage carriers. Along the way, they met members of a local indigenous group. While the guide and luggage carriers trembled with fear, Maud looked the members of this group in the eye and greeted them with a smile. She continued marching assuredly through the group while her entourage followed with trepidation. Later, she was told that these people were head-hunters and cannibals and that they normally would cook whatever live game they came upon, including humans! While we do not know with any certainty, it is quite possible that this took place as she was heading to Jiama. Wherever it took place, this is another example of Maud being courageous while trusting God to keep her safe.

Maud described her time in Jiama in her 1928 Council Report:

> I entered into new experiences at Jiama. Here I found the people different, the language different, while I had the same work, it was carried on in a different way. Sometimes I thought I was different too. In Jiama besides the hospital work, I carried 2 sewing classes a week for the school, took my turn leading the women's classes, itinerating, preaching, and prayer services. The greater part of the year I made up 17 feedings a day for motherless babies.[95]

It is indeed unfortunate that there are no known letters or diaries where Maud explained how she thought she had changed by working in Jiama. Again, we are left to wonder.

As noted in Maud's vita (which can be found at the beginning of Chapter One), on March 17, 1928, Maud became a Life Patron of the United Brethren Women's Missionary Society. The membership fee at that time was $100. Maud had either saved for several years to pay for this or possibly a church (or churches) back home raised the money as a gift for her. Life patrons became voting members of the Board of Managers, which was responsible for formulating plans and policies of the Association.

Maud left Jiama in June 1928 and headed for a six-month assignment back in Rotifunk, where she reported that she "had successes enough to cheer and encourage" her, and also had "failures enough" to keep her humble.[96] Then in July 1929, she was once again in Taiama, where she remained until she went on her furlough in June 1930. Between July and December 1929, Maud treated 4,249 patients, extracted twenty-four teeth, performed two minor operations, held fifty-nine services with 1,615 in attendance, and was in charge of the Sunday School and officiated as Postal Agent for Taiama.[97] (Whew!)

While in Taiama, another missionary, Charles W. Leader, and his wife arrived. Leader wrote a letter to a friend and stated, "We are very glad that Miss Hoyle has already arrived and will be with us for the year. We shall never forget the brightness and encouragement she gave us during her month with us during our first experience on the field when everything was so new and trying."[98]

As noted earlier, Maud, and all the medical missionaries in Sierra Leone, had to treat numerous conditions and diseases. In an article for *The Evangel* (found on the next page), she listed fifty-six of them—one for each letter in the phrase "Medical Work in Rotifunk, Taiama, and Jiama, Sierra Leone, West Africa."[99]

As the remainder of the article notes, Maud and her colleagues were following Jesus's footsteps and wanted to not only heal the people of their physical infirmities, but also to share with them the love of God.

In her book, *American Women in Mission*, Dana Lee Robert states that

> Rather than being remembered for "preaching the gospel," the quintessential 'male' task, missionary women have been noted for meeting human needs and helping others, sacrificing themselves ..., all for the sake of bringing the world to Christ.... Women's mission theory was holistic, with emphasis on both evangelism and meeting human needs.[100]

Medical Work in Rotifunk, Taiama, and Jiama, Sierra Leone, West Africa

M-alaria			
E-lephantiasis	W-orms		
D-ropsy	O-phthalmia	I-nfluenza	
I-ndigestion	R-heumatism	N-euralgia	
C-ancer	K-idney diseases		
A-sthma			
L-eprosy			
R-ickets			
O-bstetrics	T-oothache		J-aundice
T-ape-worms	A-stigmatism	A-nemia	I-nsomnia
I-tch	I-nflammations	N-ervousness	A-poplexy
F-evers	A-bscesses	D-ysentery	M-umps
U-lcers	M-easles		A-bortion
N-ose-bleed	A-ccidents		
K-ing's evil			
S-nake-bite			A-bdomen, swollen
I-nsanity	L-ock-jaw	W-hooping-cough	F-ractures
E-arache	E-yes, sore	E-pilepsy	R-upture
R-ing-worm	O-besity	S-yphilis	I-fantile-paralysis
R-ash	N-ausea	T-umors	C-onsumption
A-rthritis	E-nlarged spleen		A-lcoholism

Our medical work is made up in part by attending these and other diseases. This type of work drives the entering wedge for preaching the Gospel truths and for teaching the power of God's word. As the medical missionaries go among the people in the name and the spirit of the Great Physician, they try to follow the example set by Him who caused the blind to receive their sight, the lame to walk, the lepers to be cleansed, and the deaf to hear. I believe that these labors increased, developed, and enriched by the love of our crucified Savior will bear abundant testimony to the love of God who "so loved the world, that He gave His only begotten Son that whosoever believeth in Him should not perish, but have everlasting life." By these labors many will, therefore, come to know Him whom to know aright is life eternal.—*Maude Hoyle.*

54. Article by Maud Hoyle. *The Evangel.* Vol XLIX, No. 12 (December 1930): 336.

This matches what the pastor at Taiama, Rev. T. B. Williams, wrote in an article about Maud for *The Evangel*.[101] This article is the most detailed, first-hand description we have of Maud's medical expertise, her character, her love for the people of Sierra Leone, and her love for Christ. Rather than quoting a few sentences, the article in its entirety is included, for it is certainly well-worth reading.

Opposite page: 55. Article about Maud Hoyle. *The Evangel.* Vol XLIX, No. 10 (October 1930): 279.

thousand to twenty-five thousand dollars. These buildings are to serve the communities as centers of a varied missionary program. The board in charge of this great work will welcome generous contributions in order that the second decade of the history of the mission will be characterized by an adequate building program.
La Cygne, Kansas.

MISS MAUDE E. HOYLE
(Twelve Month's Medical Ministry at Taiama)
By Rev. T. B. Williams, Pastor at Taiama

In the early part of July, 1929, the subject of this brief sketch from Rotifunk took over the Taiama Dispensary. A most rapid, phenomenal change for the better came about. Under Nurse Hoyle's skilled and tactful handling of the situation, the adolescent Taiama Dispensary within a very short time realized its full-blown manhood. It never was thought or known that there were so many sick folks of divers diseases in the Taiama chiefdom, but when she took over crowds of sick folks came pouring in from every direction into the town for treatment. The fame of this wonderful woman, as she is generally and rightly thought to be, spread rapidly as fire among stubble into the remotest corners of the chiefdom, and far beyond its frontiers into neighboring chiefdoms. Overwhelming numbers of men, women, and children infected with yaws and leprosy, crowded into the too small waiting room of the dispensary to receive hypodermic injections which are evidently miraculous in their workings and healing.

For six months, July to December, 1929, injections were given once weekly. On Tuesdays these were given, but as the number kept increasing, injections averaging about ninety each time, besides the regular dispensing of drugs, being too strenuous and exacting upon one person, the time was changed from once a week to twice a week for injections and even then every injection day was a full day. It is of interest to note that when on these special days there is overcrowding in the waiting room—twice the size of which would hardly hold all the people—resulting in irritating and confusing noise caused by those who jostle and elbow one another to gain entrance into the dispensary, Miss Hoyle is never irritated, never loses her temper, for to her the people's noise is music, for she loves them and enjoys the task, though irksome, of relieving them of pain and disease. She never shows signs of fatigue even in the evenings of her busiest days. Her temper is always sweet; her smiles radiant and cheery. Her peculiarly humane disposition, her saintly bearing and tender, sympathetic touch indelibly impress themselves upon the memory of all who received the benefits of her service of healing from far and near.

The natives, with the possible exception of the educated class, cannot discriminate between a nurse and a doctor. They call Miss Hoyle a doctor. They are mistaken, but in her case in particular their error is reasonable and excusable for one reason that she has cured many cases that have baffled doctors. Several times I was privileged to hear the term "Baomba" (Savior, in Mendi) being applied to Miss Hoyle and she well deserves being called Savior though not in the sense of saving from sin, but she did save multitudes from the blights and ravages of disease. Very far reaching has been the influence of this woman of God—a model missionary of a fine and flawless Christ-like character. She was the idol of the little girls of Taiama for they discovered in her contact with them traits that are loving, tender, and motherly, and so they loved her tenderly and clung to her as a material demonstration of her love for the little girls. At her own expense she sewed and distributed to them over sixty dresses to put on in order to attend the church services as the majority of them had no clothing whatever. This concrete manifestation of genuine Christian love more than anything else endeared her to the hearts of the little girls and their mothers. Mothers with sick babies will not soon forget Miss Hoyle's ministeries of healing, flavored with the essence of selfless Christian love and sympathy. She never turned out a case however bad unless she found that an operation by a doctor was all that was necessary. It is regretted by the public that she did not complete her full three year term at Taiama, and it is generally felt in the community that her twelve months at Taiama were too beneficent to be so brief. Young and old, near and distant, deeply regret her departure and unanimously express the sanguine hope for her return at the expiration of her furlough.

At this writing Miss Hoyle is on the bosom of the Atlantic sailing homeward. Our prayers and good wishes go with her for a pleasant voyage and safe arrival home.

"When we believe in Jesus we know that goodness is stronger than evil, and that truth is mightier than falsehood, and that love never fails."

News of the Times

1921 – Polio epidemic continues and strikes future U.S. President Franklin D. Roosevelt.

1923 – Calvin Coolidge becomes President after the sudden death of Warren G. Harding.

1924 – Joseph Stalin gains control of Soviet Union.

1925 – Scopes "Monkey Trial" begins.

1927 – Lindbergh makes the first nonstop solo trans-Atlantic flight in his Spirit of St. Louis.

1927 – The Jazz Singer is the first full-length talking picture to achieve success.

1928 – Herbert Hoover elected President.

1928 – Penicillin is discovered.

1928 – Walt Disney's Steamboat Willie introduces Mickey Mouse to the world.

1929 – The U.S. stock market crashes, causing the beginning of the Great Depression.

1930 – 3M employee Richard Drew invents Scotch Tape.

1930 – As Depression worsens, 1,350 banks in the US fail, and the federal government begins the Public Works program.

A few of the active artists, musicians, and writers at this time: Picasso, Chagall, Stravinsky, Hoagy Carmichael, Irving Berlin, F. Scott Fitzgerald, Hemingway, Faulkner.

Chapter Eight:
Finishing the Race

> *I have fought the good fight,*
> *I have finished the race,*
> *I have kept the faith.*
> —2 Timothy 4:7 (NIV)

Maud left Sierra Leone for her third furlough, arriving in New York on the *Baltic* on July 21, 1930.[102] She again spent much time speaking at various United Brethren churches in the Midwest, traveling as far as Bloomington, Illinois to be the main speaker at the Second United Brethren Church on September 12, 1930.[103]

56. Maud and her mother Ida

Much to Maud's disappointment, cataracts were forming on her eyes and her vision grew so bad that she was forced to make the decision not to return to the mission field as scheduled.[104] She must have been extremely disappointed not to be going back to the people she loved in Sierra Leone. At the same time, she undoubtedly was grateful that she was now available to care for her mother who was blind and failing in health. Maud once again settled back at the "Hoyle Homestead" on Columbus Avenue in Springfield.

Maud continued to speak at churches whenever asked. We know, for example, that in the fall of 1931, she spoke at Yankeetown (Indiana) United Brethren one week[105] and a few weeks later she was the principle speaker at the Institute of the Missionary Society of the Newcastle-Richmond (Indiana) district of the United Brethren Church.[106]

At some point, Maud had surgery to remove her cataracts which restored her sight.[107] The surgeon, Dr. Perley H. Kilbourne, of Dayton, Ohio, was a devout member of the United Brethren Church. According to an oft-repeated family story, Dr. Kilbourne would not accept any money for performing the surgery. So, Maud offered him a leopard skin that she had brought back from Africa. It had been killed just outside her bedroom window. Maud had it mounted on green felt which matched its green, glass eyes.

When Maud returned home, the country was in the midst of the Great Depression. Although she was fortunate to receive a small pension from the church, it was barely enough to support her and her mother. Maud's great-niece, Susan Hoyle Lizza, remembers hearing the story that Maud was reluctant to accept any help, since everyone she knew was also suffering financially. Her brothers, Walter and Wilbur, worked around this by often leaving a dollar inside Maud's Bible when they visited their mother and sister. They knew that she would find the money there. Although she had little, she was always very generous. For example, later, in 1942, Maud used her rations to purchase for her niece, Dorothy, her first pair of white nurse's shoes after she had graduated from nurse's training.

Maud lovingly took care of her mother until July 27, 1936, the day Ida died. Ida was buried in a plain black dress. Maud's one regret was that she did not have enough money to purchase a white collar to put on the dress, as was the custom of the time.

The Missionary Society of Columbus Avenue Church held a memorial service for Ida. Part of the obituary included in the program focused on Ida's joy of Maud's service as a missionary:

> A proving time came in her life, scarcely two years after the death of her husband. The Lord was calling her only daughter to become a foreign missionary. By the time Maud sailed for Africa in 1921, Mother Hoyle had yielded her will to God's will and was so happy to be accounted worthy to have a daughter to carry the Gospel to the heathen. She would gladly have gone herself would it have been possible. During the years her daughter's stay in Africa, Mrs. Hoyle's earnest prayers and interest were for the work there, in fact, she fairly lived in Africa in her spirit. However, her interest in Columbus Ave. Church never abated even unto the last.

Maud's life changed once again after her mother's death. She knew that she felt called to continue ministering to people by caring for the sick. She also knew that it was impractical for her to continue living at the family home on Columbus Avenue. She decided to take a job as a nurse at the Ohio Masonic Home, located in Springfield, where she also was provided room and board.

57. Masonic home and Rickly Memorial Hospital, Springfield, Ohio.

The Masonic Home, which is still in operation today, had opened in 1895. It was originally for the elderly Ohio Masons, especially those with few assets, and their wives, widows, or orphans. Maud worked there from 1936–1940. According to the 1940 Census, she worked 52 hours/week and her annual salary was $720.[108]

The Columbus Avenue Church remained an important part of Maud's life and she continued to be admired and respected by members of the church. In 1936, the women of the church's Ladies' Aid Society, gave Maud a quilt that they had made during the past year as a fundraising project. People paid ten cents to have a name inscribed on the quilt. In the end, there were 424 names which were embroidered as a labor of love by Maud's niece, Helen, daughter of Wilbur and Etta Hoyle. An article about this quilt appeared in the *Springfield News & Sun* in a column, "From the Window," written by Anna Marie Tennant:

> Have you ever dreamed about darkest Africa, of how sometimes you might like to tour there? A Springfield woman, the Rev. Maud Hoyle, of Columbus Av., was a former missionary in that country. Many are the tales she tells of the weird customs which prevail there. Miss Hoyle is now a nurse in the Ohio Masonic Home hospital. At a recent meeting of the Ladies' Aid Society of the Columbus Avenue United Brethren Church of which she is a member, the members honored her in a unique way. For more than one year, these members have been working on a name quilt and secured 400 names and more of citizens of Springfield and Clark County, many of whom are known to Miss Hoyle personally. After the quilt was completed, the society decided to give it to Miss Hoyle, who was the first pastor of the Columbus Avenue Church. I am under the impression that she is also the second regularly installed woman pastor of any local church, the first I believe being Miss Henrietta Moore, pastor of the First Universalist Church.
>
> Information which comes to me states that Miss Hoyle was also the organizer of the Columbus Avenue Church. The quilt was presented to Miss Hoyle with special ceremonies on behalf of the society by Mrs. Eula Carol Martin, who used the word of the following original poem, titled 'Memories.'
>
> Lest you should be losing
> Some time in years to come,
> The names of friends and loved ones,
> When you're far away from home.
> We pieced a 'friendship quilt' to help you
> Bring back those memories,
> Of dawn, dusks, of sunsets.
>
> Each name is linked with these.
> Some day sort them out and tag them.
> And file each name away,
> In your heart for future reference,
> Until some reminiscent day.
> You'll see the names of some who were present
> When they broke the ground of the church.

And that has been some twenty-four years
If back in your memory you'll search.
And you were called as their pastor
And there are names linked with thee,
Some are still members, others have gone
And some still your friends to be.
But this little church by the wayside
Has many a fond memory.

And the bell in the belfry still beckons
To give new hope to thee.
So from our hearts, we are wishing you,
Success in your work; dreams come true.
Memories to borrow; memories to lend;
And more of love than you can spend.[109]

The quilt is now at the Clark County Historical Society. Here are some photos of it with closeups of a few of the Hoyle names that were included.

58. Friendship Quilt

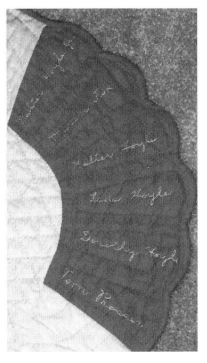
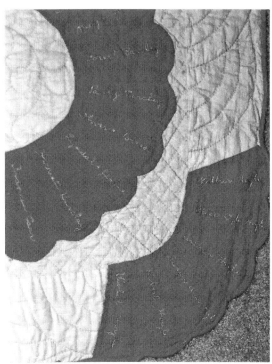

59. Maud outside Rickly Hospital, Ohio Masonic Home.

Maud left the Masonic Home to begin work as a private duty nurse, taking care of two elderly sisters in Dayton, Ohio. The sisters, Edith M. Stevens and Fannie R. McCrosson, lived at 1727 W. 1st Street. There is no information about these sisters that informs us how they happened to hire Maud. It is possible that they were involved with the United Brethren Church and either knew or knew about Maud through church contacts. She worked for them from 1941 until October 1944, when Edith Stevens passed away.

Maud's official status in the United Brethren Church for the years 1931–1943 was "Itinerate Elder" with the designation that she was "on furlough" for the years 1931–1938. In 1944, her official ministerial status was changed to "Local Elder." This designation was given to those ministers "who for any reason were without ministerial employment."[110] At the age of 63, it was unlikely that she would be a full-time minister at a church again. She was also deeply committed to nursing, and in January 1945, Maud began working at the Otterbein Home in Lebanon, Ohio as a nurse. As with the Masonic Home, Maud (and most of the employees) lived on site.

The Otterbein Home was established in 1912 as the United Brethren Orphanage and Home for the Aged. (Its name was changed to the Otterbein Home during the 1913 General Conference[111]). The United Brethren purchased 4,000 acres and fifty buildings of a former Shaker settlement, called Union Village, to create this

60. Marble Hall, Otterbein Home, circa 1960. Image from MidPointe Digital Archives, www.MidPointeDigitalArchive.org.

home. The contract to buy the land was signed in Marble Hall which was built by the Shakers in 1810 and is the one of the few Shaker buildings on the grounds still standing today. The Otterbein Home continues to thrive today as a retirement community under the auspices of the United Methodist Church.

Friends and family visiting Maud at the Otterbein Home would spend time in the lounge of the medical building or in her apartment.

61. Main lounge, Medical Building, Otterbein Home. Image from MidPointe Digital Archives, www.MidPointeDigitalArchive.org

62. Typical Room, Otterbein Home, c. 1960. Image from MidPointe Digital Archives, www.MidPointeDigitalArchive.org

Many missionaries retired to the Otterbein Home. Maud must have been delighted to reconnect with the friends she had made while in Sierra Leone, including Miss Vesper. Below is a photo of some of the former missionaries to Sierra Leone, taken in 1951, when Rev. and Mrs. Ferguson of West Africa were visiting Otterbein Home.

63. Missionaries at the Otterbein Home, 1951. From left to right: Miss McKinzie, Miss Vesper, Mrs. Ferguson, Rev. Ferguson, Mrs. Musselman, and Miss Hoyle. (Miss Vesper returned to Sierra Leone a few months after this photo was taken)

Maud ministered to her patients at the Otterbein Home, providing loving and skillful nursing care. She would often check on her critically-ill patients during the night, even after having worked all day. In 1955, at the age of 74, she was appointed temporary Director of the Hospital.[112] The administration must have been impressed with Maud's abilities to offer her the position, and Maud, true to form, willingly accepted any opportunity to be of service.

Maud applied for, and received, membership at the Otterbein Home in February 1952. This meant that when Maud was no longer able to work, she would automatically become a resident/patient. This transition from employee to resident took place on January 1, 1957.

64. Nurses at the Otterbein Home, 1957. Maud is in the front row, second from left.

After she retired, Maud would often relieve other nurses whenever needed. She had congestive heart failure, which often caused her feet to swell to the point that at times she could not put on her shoes. This,

65. Maud outside Columbus Avenue Church, circa 1950.

however, did not deter her. She was known to tie handkerchiefs around her feet as she prepared to go to a dying patient's room to sit with them at night so that they would not die alone. She would slip back to her bedroom before the supervisor came on duty in the morning so that she wouldn't be caught working when she should have been caring for herself.

During these long nights, she would often crochet. One time, she sat with a patient on a Saturday night and began crocheting an afghan. In the early hours of Sunday morning, she realized that she had been crocheting on the Sabbath, something that she felt was wrong to do if she were to keep the Sabbath holy. So, she ripped all her stitches out to re-do another day.

Maud would also assist the pastor in serving Holy Communion in the hospital at the Otterbein Home. It was noted that others found it "an inspiration to see her in her ministration of the sacraments to the invalids and ill patients."[113]

During the time that Maud lived at Otterbein, she would frequently visit family and friends in Springfield. Whenever she was there, she would attend services at the Columbus Avenue Church.

Maud came to Springfield when her brother, Wilbur, passed away in 1948, and when brother Walter, was dying in 1953. Her niece, Dorothy Hoyle Cash, remembers that Maud sat with Walter for hours. She also assured Dorothy that she had been a good daughter. Having Maud's approval meant so much to Dorothy.

Another time that Maud went to Springfield was in July 1958. She went there to take care of her sister-in-law, Henrietta Fissell Hoyle (Wilbur's widow), who was recovering from surgery for a ruptured gall bladder. John Hoyle (Wilbur's grandson), gave the following account of his remembrances of July 12, 1958:

> It was at 119 N. Belmont, in the living room where Aunt Maud had a heart attack. My father (Paul) got a call that Aunt Maud was sick, and Dad and I rushed over there. We were about seven or eight blocks away. Aunt Maud was on the sofa and not conscious but still breathing. Her skin was beginning to turn blue. I went to the phone and called the fire department and asked that the emergency squad be sent. When they arrived, they gave her oxygen and called for a funeral home ambulance to take her to the hospital as the ride would be smoother. It came quickly and transported her

to Springfield City Hospital. The young doctor in the emergency room said that they tried to save her, but it was not possible.

Dorothy Hoyle Cash, remembers that the doctor wanted to perform an autopsy because Maud was from out-of-town. Dorothy's brothers, Arthur and Walter, drove to Lebanon to get a report from Maud's doctor stating that she had suffered from heart disease for years so that an autopsy was not necessary.

66. Maud's Death Certificate.

While her family and friends mourned their loss, they also remembered the many times she had told them, "What a glorious day it will be when I will be reunited with Ma, Pa, and the boys."

Maud's funeral service was held on July 15, 1958 at the church she had founded on Columbus Avenue. She was buried on the family plot at Newcomer's Cemetery in Springfield, next to her parents and sister Lottie.

In speaking at the Annual Conference for the Evangelical United Brethren Church, Rev. Ira C. Clark of the Otterbein Home, said of Maud:

> This faithful and effectual worker and servant of the Lord lived and labored for others, in a self-forgetful manner, as an angel of mercy and a witness for her Saviour... Through the arms of sympathy and tender love of this great servant of Christ, many persons in need of physical or spiritual healing found it. Truly a mother of Israel has fallen.[114]

67. Maud's marker, Newcomer Cemetery.

Maud's journey was over; she had fought the good fight and finished the race. She most certainly had kept the faith. Her entire life was devoted to service and to sharing the good news of God's love. Indeed, she had beautiful feet.

News of the Times

1931–1939

1931 – Empire State Building in New York City opens.
1931 – Star Spangled Banner (written in 1814) becomes official U.S. national anthem.
1932 – Franklin D. Roosevelt elected President.
1932 – Dust Bowl begins in Great Plains
1933 – Hitler becomes chancellor of Germany
1933 – Prohibition is repealed in U.S.
1936 – China and Japan enter into a war that will continue through World War II.
1936 – King Edward VIII abdicates British throne to marry the American Wallis Simpson.
1938 – Germany invades Austria; first Jews are sent to concentration camps.
1939 – Germany invades Poland; World War II begins.

A few of the active artists, musicians, performers, and writers at this time: Jean Sibelius, Duke Ellington, Charlie Chaplin, Marlene Detrick, James Cagney, Virginia Woolf, William Faulkner, Pearl S. Buck.

1940–1949

1941 – Japanese attack the U.S. at Pearl Harbor.
1944 – Normandy is invaded by the Allied Forces on what will be known as D-Day
1944 – Harry S. Truman becomes President after Franklin Roosevelt dies
1945 – U.S. drops atomic bombs on Hiroshima and Nagasaki.
1945 – World War II comes to an end and the United Nations is formed.
1948 – Ghandi is assassinated.
1949 – Chairman Mao forms the "Communist People's Republic of China".

A few of the active artists, musicians, performers, and writers at this time: Matisse, Georgia O'Keeffe, Copland, Prokofiev, Irving Berlin, Glenn Miller, Greta Garbo, Alfred Hitchcock, C. S. Lewis, E. B. White, Agatha Christie.

1950–1958

1950 – Korean War begins.

1952 – Dwight D. Eisenhower is elected President.

1953 – Joseph Stalin dies.

1954 – U.S. Supreme Court rules in the Brown vs Board of Education that racial segregation in public schools is unconstitutional.

1955 – Disneyland opens in Anaheim, California.

1956 – Martin Luther King, Jr., organizes boycott of Montgomery, Alabama public transportation.

1958 – U.S. launched Explorer I, the first American satellite, into Earth's orbit.

A few of the active artists, musicians, performers, and writers at this time: Picasso, Jackson Pollock, Stravinsky, Dave Brubeck, Hoagy Carmichael, Elvis Presley, Katharine Hepburn, Cary Grant, Bob Hope, Dr. Seuss, Thurber, Salinger.

Epilogue

I am now at the end of my journey of researching and writing about Aunt Maud's remarkable life. Before closing, though, I wanted to take some time to reflect on what I have learned about Aunt Maud as a person and what impact her story has had on me.

The first thing that I will mention is that by finishing this project, I have, at long last, fulfilled a promise that I made to my mother, Dorothy Hoyle Cash, to write Aunt Maud's story. I wish that I would have completed this while my mother was still alive. She would have shared my excitement as I discovered new details about Aunt Maud's life. And I know that she would be pleased that Aunt Maud's story is finally being told.

I also want to state that I am aware that my account of Aunt Maud seems to describe a nearly perfect person. Even though that is how our family viewed her, we, obviously, know that she was human. She undoubtedly had flaws. However, I could only write what I could document. If, through my research, we had found any of Aunt Maud's diaries or letters to family or close friends, we might have a glimpse of her feelings about all that she experienced. We might know of any times when her faith in God may have wavered or whether she was ever afraid, or how she viewed the world. Although we don't have those pieces of her life, I feel confident in saying that whatever faults she had, whatever doubts she experienced, she, through her faith in God, was able to overcome them. This enabled her to accomplish all the good that she did. Staying faithful and conquering whatever weaknesses she may have had are part of what make Aunt Maud's life so inspirational to me.

My research into her life has allowed me to learn more about Aunt Maud's character. Clearly, she was a strong, determined woman. She never seemed to hesitate to pursue whatever she felt called to do, whether it was applying for seminary, even though she did not possess the stated requirements, or applying to become a missionary, in spite of being the age at which most female missionaries were sent back home. Aunt Maud also possessed confidence as evidenced in her seeking approval for and then overseeing the building of a new church, which she then pastored. This she did, even though she was a young and inexperienced woman at a time when women didn't even have the right to vote. No matter the obstacles, Aunt Maud always followed wherever God led her.

Courage was another of Aunt Maud's attributes. She went to live in a country that was completely unknown to her, where she had to learn new languages and new customs, and where she faced dangers of wild animals, and even headhunters. Although she had studied nursing, she certainly was confronted with diseases and illnesses that she had never encountered before. Yet, she never hesitated to care for the people who needed her. Indeed, she was considered one of the most skilled nurses in Sierra Leone, one who could cure diseases even doctors could not.

Aunt Maud was also responsive and was always willing to do whatever or to go wherever she was needed. When she went to Sierra Leone, it was to serve as a medical missionary. However, once there, she was also asked to teach and to be a surrogate mother, tasks for which she was unprepared. Nevertheless, she willingly accepted these, and any other responsibility asked of her. Also, as noted in her story, there were times she was given only a few hours' notice to pack and prepare to move to a new mission station. Her answer to any call for help seemed to be a resounding YES!

In the thesis that Aunt Maud wrote in seminary, she discussed the idea that true religion is its power to help, to relieve suffering, and to transform lives. The first sermon she gave at the Columbus Avenue United Brethren

Church, examined the belief that a good life, one of service, is the most powerful preaching. Aunt Maud lived what she preached. Her love and compassion for all people showed through her many actions.

Mostly, as I have noted often throughout this book, Aunt Maud's strongest character trait was her faithfulness to God. She trusted God to open doors, to lead her to the right pathways, and to protect her. She fully surrendered to herself to God and she spent her life serving others in Christ's name. Through her, others could see the Good News lived and could hear the Good News proclaimed.

Aunt Maud's story is one of an amazing woman. She may never have been destined for greatness that would be recorded in history books, but that does not make her any less remarkable. I believe that my great aunt, Maud Elizabeth Hoyle, was extraordinary for the way that she loved and touched the lives of her family and of the many people to whom she ministered—from those in the poor, rural church that she pastored, to the citizens of Sierra Leone, to the dying she cared for in a nursing home. Her life is a testimony that can speak to generations about a woman who walked with God every step of her life.

What a wonderful legacy she has left us!

Part Two: Maud's Writings

Thesis
Practical Christianity
Maud Elizabeth Hoyle

(This was in a notebook with "Thesis" written on the cover. It is most likely a copy of the thesis that Maud wrote in 1909 as a graduation requirement from Bonebrake Theological Seminary.)

> Be strong!
> We are not here to play, to dream, to drift,
> We have hard work to do, and loads to lift,
> Shun not the struggle, face it; 'tis God's gift.
>
> Be strong!
> It matters not how deep entrenched the wrong,
> How hard the battle goes, the day how long.
> Faint not, fight on! Tomorrow comes the song.
> —Maltbie D. Babcock, D. D.

The test of true religion is its power to help men, to relieve suffering, to transform the lives of men.

C. E. Jefferson says that Christianity is nothing, according to the writers of the New Testament, unless it moves in the realm of power.

Jesus in his first reported sermon defined his mission. He came to Nazareth, his childhood home, went into the pulpit on the Sabbath day, found and read from Isaiah: "The Spirit of the Lord is upon me, because he anointed me to preach good tidings to the poor; He hath sent me to proclaim release to the captives, And recovering of sight to the blind. To set at liberty them that are bruised, To proclaim the acceptable year of the Lord." He had come, he said, to fulfill this prophecy; this was his mission. A year or so later he appointed twelve apostles to take up the work which he could not complete without help, and this was the commission he gave to them: "As ye go, preach; saying, The kingdom of heaven is at hand. Heal the sick, raise the dead, cleanse the lepers, cast out devils; freely ye received, freely give."

The function of the Christian Church is *to teach* us how to live; it is *to bring* us into Christ's school, and make us his pupils. It is to receive the spirit of Christ and to continue Christ's work. It is *to carry* to men the glad tidings of sin forgiven and life bestowed. It is *to teach* us how to follow Christ; it is *to prepare* men for the coming of the kingdom of God—the kingdom of righteousness and peace and joy in holiness of spirit. It is to carry to its completion the work which Christ said he had come to initiate—*to preach* glad tidings to the poor, to heal the broken-hearted, to bring recovering of sight to the blind and liberty to the captives. It is living soberly, righteously, godly, and hopefully; it is faith, hope and love. It is the spirit of vision, of aspiration, of good will. It is in loving men as Christ loved me; and it is carrying out in our lives the spirit of the apostles' teaching. "He laid down his life for us, and we ought to lay down our lives for the brethren." But just to believe, this is not Christianity. Christianity is the spirit of Christ, the spirit of love, and service, and self-sacrifice. "He that hath not the spirit of Christ is none of his."

The Church has been too apt to think that Christ came to prepare men on the earth for a celestial happiness in heaven. It has been too apt to preach a religion that prepared men to die rather than a religion which fitted them to live. What Christ proposes to his followers is that they combine in undertaking to establish on the earth a new social order by imbuing society with a new spirit—a spirit of righteousness or square-dealing, which will lead every man to treat his neighbor as he would wish to be treated; a spirit of peace and good will, which will substitute co-operation for competition and brotherhood for mutual hostility, and, instead of "every man for himself," "in honor preferring one another."

This religion of Christ and that which we profess, can we make it practical, or, is it capable of being turned to account? The life of Jesus was consecrated for service—service for others. His was a life whose Christianity was not only passive, but it was practical. He did anything that his hands found to do. Nothing was below his notice, or his interest. He came to do his father's will. He healed the sick, opened the eyes of the blind, caused the deaf to hear, made the lame to walk, cleansed the lepers, fed the hungry, gave a kind word here, a helping hand there, and he also raised the dead to life.

And now his work is to be carried on by his people who represent him on earth. Christ tells us that those who believe in him shall do greater works than he, and it is true that, through his followers, more is being accomplished than it was possible for him to do in Palestine. The kindly feeling, the desire to help, and the increased skill that spring up under Christianity as flowers and fruits that grow in the sunshine have made Christ's work through his people greater than those he wrought on earth. They are not miracles, but are better than the power of miracles, as the prolonged sunshine is better than a flash of lightening. Blind asylums have opened many eyes and caused people to read and work even without sight. Hospitals have cured and cared for multitudes of sick and insane. We cannot raise the dead to life, but the average length of life has been greatly increased. The day laborer has more of the best things in the world—books, libraries, churches, railroads, telegraphs, newspapers—than kings have in heathen lands.

We have found out that a universal religion demands a world-wide proclamation. This great truth was but slowly apprehended, even by the apostles. The Church of Christ has not yet fully measured its obligation, growing out of its possession of a gospel adapted to and designed for the whole human race. Under the Old Testament dispensation there were predictions of "a light to lighten the Gentiles," and a "king in Zion who should have dominion from the river even unto the ends of the earth." Yet, in spite of these intimations of the world-wide reach of the Messiah's rule, the Jewish people appear to have had no thought of attempting to convert other nations to their faith. It would seem as if the instructions of Christ, crowned by his last command to "Go into all the world and make disciples of all the nations" could not have failed to convince his disciples of their obligations; and yet we find Peter, even after Pentecost, doubting whether it would be right for him to preach the gospel to a Roman centurion who had sent for him for instruction. And not until a new and extraordinary vision was given him from heaven did Peter learn that God had called the Gentiles to repentance unto life. But before the death of the apostles, the breadth of the Saviour's command was apprehended by them and the gospel was preached throughout Asia Minor, Macedonia, and Greece.

We will pass by the few centuries between with just a few remarks. The persecutions that occurred during the three centuries after Christ did not hinder the earnest propagation of the faith. In the fourth and fifth centuries, missionary operations were carried forward with much vigor. Up to the tenth century, there seems to have been a clear recognition of the obligation of all Christians to give the gospel to those who had it not.

But with the increasing obscuration of Bible doctrine and the increasing declension in Christian life, missionary activity, which had been growing more and more external, came gradually to a standstill in the fourteenth century. But thanks be to God that the light shineth in the darkness though the darkness apprehended it not.

The era of **modern missions** may properly be said to have begun in 1705. In the United States, various bodies began to plan for missionary work, but their attention was directed largely to the first inhabitants of the country who lived near them. But the work has grown, and besides the various Foreign Missionary Societies there are at least forty Women's Bands in the United States having not less than thirty-three thousand auxiliaries, including Children's Bands with a membership estimated at about seven hundred thousand. And the good that they are doing in advancing Christ's kingdom here on earth, God only knows.

In heathen lands, the helps that we have here do not exist and, therefore, the missionary must create them. He must found not only churches, but schools, hospitals, printing presses, kindergartens, orphanages, and the various other kinds of Christian and benevolent work carried on in our country. He must train up a native ministry, erect buildings, translate and print books, tracts, and catechisms.

In some lands, the missionary must even teach the men how to make clothing, to build houses, to cultivate the soil, while his wife shows the women how to sew and to cook and to care for their children and to make decent homes. Thus, the foreign missionary is obliged to unite the adaptability of a jack-of-all-trades to the function of an archbishop.

There is practical work done among the lepers. And it is to Christianity that we are indebted for the attempt to relieve those sufferers and to make them a self-sustaining community. In India, these settlements are carried on at several places, and others are found in China, Japan, Madagascar, Africa, South America, the Philippines, Sumatra, and also Great Britain and the United States.

The great end of Christian missions is without doubt to make known to all mankind the Gospel of the grace of

God, that Gospel which brings salvation. To save the soul from death through faith in Him who is the Savior of all men, this is the high aim and great justification of all missionary effort; nothing short of this will ever satisfy the true servant of Christ. But this supreme object of Christian missions always has been best accomplished in connection with efforts for the temporal good of the people among whom they labor. Indeed, did Christianity not bring temporal as well as spiritual blessings, we might well doubt its Divine origin, and whether it was really adapted to mankind.

Missionary work brings good to heathen peoples in many directions and exerts a beneficent influence as the great civilizing, educational, philanthropic, and healing power in many parts of the world.

As has been stated, Christianity was clouded during the Middle Ages, and when modern missions commenced, was but dimly realized. Yet Carey, who went to India to preach salvation from sin, immediately set about abolishing the suttee [sati]. Verbeck, of Japan, thought his time well spent in teaching English and in imparting the Christian conception of national life to the company of young men who afterward led their empire in its wonderous advance to a high place among the civilized nations of the world.

The gospel of a clean shirt went side by side with that of repentance in the South Seas and Africa. Wherever the missionary has gone, his message has been addressed to the intellect as well as to the heart, and he has sought to provide a clean body and comfortable home for the soul that would grow into the purity of the Christian life.

It is a matter of great moment for the welfare of the world that more than eighteen thousand men and women are devoting themselves with singleness of purpose, and often in great privation, to the uplifting of the lives of the ignorant and degraded in what are still the dark places of the earth. Let us turn for a moment to those departments which so many have hitherto considered the adjuncts to missionary work, but which are today assuming their proper place in the front rank.

Education naturally leads. These eighteen thousand missionaries have over one million pupils under instruction, the great majority in the elementary and village day schools, but a goodly number in those of higher rank. Closely allied to direct education is the furnishing of a pure and elevating literature. And few departments of science have made such strides, of late years, as **medicine**. Closely allied to the medical is the reformatory and **philanthropic work** with its three hundred orphanages and foundling asylums, its one hundred leper homes, thirty institutions for the blind and deaf, one hundred and sixty refuges for rescue work, the opium slave and the insane.

Let us now for a time turn our attention to some other things that have been accomplished in Christ's name. We have at times turned our backs on the **Salvation Army**, never thinking of what good they were doing. It was when but a mere child that William Booth, seeing the degradation and helpless misery of the poor stockingers of his native town, wandering gaunt and hungry, stricken through the streets droning out their melancholy ditties, crowding the Union or toiling like galley slaves on relief works for a bare subsistence, kindled in his heart yearnings to help that class of people. He has, with God's help and by the aid of his followers, done a great deal in lessening the miseries of this class of people, and not only brought heavenly hopes and earthly gladness to the hearts of multitudes of these wretched crowds, but also many material blessings, including such common-place things as food, raiment, home, and work, the parent of so many other temporal benefits.

It was a stupendous undertaking, but Mr. Booth had the pluck and stick-to-itiveness that knows no defeat. He formed colonies. The city colony has depots and within each, there are two departments, one dealing with food, the other with shelter. Of these both are worked together and minister to the same individuals. Many come for food who do not come for shelter, although most of those who come for shelter, also come for food, which is sold on terms to cover, as nearly as possible, the cost price and working expenses of the establishment. These cheap food depots, I have no doubt, have been and are of great service to numbers of hungry, starving men, women, and children, at such low prices which must be within the reach of all, except the absolute penniless. But it is the shelter that I regard as the most useful feature in this part of their undertaking, for if anything is to be done to get hold of those who use the depot, some more favorable opportunity must be afforded than is offered by the mere coming into the food store to get, perhaps, only a bowl of soup.

By eight o'clock in the evenings, the shelter is pretty well filled, two or three hundred men in the men's shelter or as many women in the women's shelter, are collected together (most of them are strangers to each other) in a large room. They are all wretchedly poor. Now, a religious service is held. The girls have their banjos and their tambourines, and for a couple of hours there are prayers short and to the point; there are addresses, some delivered by the leaders of the meeting, but most of the testimonies are of those who have been saved at previous meetings, and who rising in their seats, tell their companions of their experience.

The meeting over, the girls go to the training home while the men remain all night. In the morning, they have their breakfast, and, after a short service, go off their various ways. In some places, they have it so that they can wash their clothing and have them clean for the next day. In this way, they will be more likely to find employment.

For ones that come to them without money to pay for food and shelter in the larger cities, they have Industrial workshops, where in exchange for work done by them, they are fed and sheltered until they can procure work for themselves, or it can be found for them elsewhere.

No smoking, drinking, bad language, or conduct calculated to demoralize is permitted on the factory premises. No one under the influence of drink is admitted. And anyone refusing to work, or guilty of bad conduct, is required to leave the premises.

And still another department of this city colony is the household salvage brigade. This is a civil force of organized collectors, who patrol the whole town as regularly as the policeman, who have their appointed beats, of which we all know something, though, perhaps we have donated and then never given it another thought. That is when collectors of the Army call at your door for old clothing, shoes, papers, magazines, etc. Have you ever given it a thought what they do with these?

The collection is taken say, once or twice a week or more frequently, according to the season and circumstances. The collection is transferred to depots as central as possible in the different districts. Already in some provincial towns a great business is done by the conversion of old shoes into new. They call the men so employed "translators." Boots and shoes, as we all know, do not go to pieces all at once, or, in all parts at once. The sole often wears out utterly, while the upper leather is quite good, or vice versa. A couple of thousand of these pairs of boots and shoes are taken, and he is a terrible poor cobbler or has a terrible poor lot of shoes and boots to work on if he cannot construct at least five hundred pairs which, if not quite good, will be immeasurably better than the apologies for boots which cover the feet of many a poor tramp, to say nothing of the number of poor children who are at the present time attending our public schools.

This is, however, only one branch of industry. They do the same with old umbrellas as well as with shoes. They collect old bottles, wash and sort them, and send them out on a new lease of life. This alone keeps a considerable number of people going. And then, as to the literature, after the magazine has been read by its owner, it is passed on to the reading rooms, work houses, and hospitals. Thus, it is enjoyed by many people who otherwise would never see it. They also have rescue homes, retreats for inebriates, homes for discharged prisoners, enquiry offices for the discovery of lost friends and relatives, and the advice bureau. These names will suffice to designate the practical Christian work they are doing on other lines. Their farm colonies are also a great help in transforming the lives of men.

The Salvation Army's flag flies in fifty-six countries. Russia is being opened up to them now. They have 8,841 societies; their preachers preach in fifty-six different languages. They have 21,025 chief officers, 4,000 employees, 51,161 local officers. There are 19,683 men playing in their musical bands. The Army publishes sixty-nine periodicals and thirty newspapers in twenty-five different languages, with an annual circulation of 1,013,292 copies. Through these they have found 3,000 missing persons in one year and found employment for 85,000 more. They shelter 2,862 by night and feed 9,977,241 by day. They have 160 slum posts. Twenty-one slum posts are in the United States. They have founded fifteen farm colonies.

The **Volunteers of America** is another organization we hear so much about on account of their practical Christian work. Some prisoners in San Quentin, California, wrote a letter asking Maud Ballington Booth to visit them during her stay in San Francisco. This visit left such a deep impression on her heart and she longed for an opportunity to practically help the prisoners. She did not attempt to preach, for undoubtedly their consciences in many a dark lonely hour had preached far more pointedly than she could. But instead, as far as possible, she tried to carry them away from prison.

At that time, she and her husband were leaders of the movement of the Salvation Army in America. But the league, known as the Volunteers of America, has nothing to do with the Salvation Army; it is in no way connected with it and is absolutely dissimilar in method and government.

This organization started in two small rooms in the Bible House, with half a dozen workers to help them, and absolutely no capital or source of income for the work that opened out before them; the Volunteers had many difficulties to face, but God's hand was with them, and they have accomplished much good.

The prison work is but one branch of their work. In 1896, in New York City, the initial meeting was held, and from that place and hour, it has grown and widened until now the movement has attained national proportions.

The call came from prison after prison. Sometimes it was a plea sent from the boys by the chaplain with his request for a visit added in earnest words. Sometimes it came from a warden who had heard the testimony of other wardens as to what had been accomplished in their prisons.

The Volunteers saw that the prisoners needed friendship and the touch of human sympathy far more than preaching or argument. Then, too, there was a large correspondence carried on with those who cared to write. In this way, they got an insight into their lives.

When men began to take the decisive step and to show their earnestness, a league was formed to which such ones, when they joined, were given a certificate of membership, a small white button with a blue star in the center, and the motto of the League in red lettering, "Look up and Hope." Of course, the Volunteers lay the greatest stress on the need of Divine help, but their labors in the prisons are not mere evangelizing efforts.

The Volunteers varied work is performed through these instrumentalities:

1. Homes for unfortunate and destitute men;
2. Homes or hotels for working men, where over 250,000 men are lodged during the year;
3. Homes of Mercy, where all young women are welcomed without distinction of creed or condition of life, and employment is found for them;
4. Homes for deserted children where between 350 - 400 are cared for during the year;
5. Prison work as has been mentioned;
6. Tenement work.

A home has been secured in Newark, New Jersey, for young women leaving prison; and another large poor man's hotel, furnished throughout, has been opened to accommodate three hundred men in Chicago; a new social wing has been added in Joliet; while a magnificent Home has been purchased on Long Island, containing ten acres of ground for discharged prisoners.

Thus, in addition to the many thousands fed on holiday occasions, thousands of homeless and shelterless are house and helped. The prison work throughout the country is becoming a known and recognized success, not only within the prison walls, but among the many who turn to them for help on leaving the prisons.

If Christianity means anything, it means all that these organizations are doing, and still more. If it is not here to make men better, to make them brothers, if it lacks the power to do that—it would be better that every lofty church spire in the land be laid low.

Love to God and love to men transfigure the commonest service as a gray and dreary cloud is transfigured by the rays of the setting sun. Much that a mother does for her child, a doctor or nurse for his patient, is very lowly service that would be hard and repulsive, but for love. It was such service that has made the names of Florence Nightingale, John Howard, and many others shine like stars in the sky.

The labors of Miss Nightingale have led to the formation of the **Red Cross Association**, which had its origin when nine years after the Crimean War, she was called to the scenes of Oriental conflict. In February 1863, at a meeting of the Société Genevoise, a proposal was made by Henry Dumont, who had witnessed the horrors of Italian battlefields. Dumont wondered whether it would not be possible in time of peace to form societies for the relief of the wounded when war should again break out.

It has caused all nations to see more fully the cruelty and horrors of war and has tended toward the settlement of national difficulties by arbitration, rather than by arms, thus, indirectly, furthering peace and unity among nations. Even outside of the miseries of war, this organization has for its prime object the relief of suffering. Muskets and cannon may be silent for a while, but the warring elements of fire, water, and wind may cause suffering at any time. With this in view, there has been added to the original what is called the American amendment. At Washington, D. C., a field agent is stationed who visits, in person, every place where aid is rendered.

The work of the Red Cross has been accomplished quietly and without ostentation. All the relief has been administered, not as charity, but as God sent. This association was formed during the winter of 1880–81. But like all other such enterprises, it had to prove itself. Not long after, the organization news of "Half the State of Michigan on Fire" called them to action on their own laws of civil relief. The agents remained on the field until the suffering was relieved. The following year, 1883, a disastrous rise in the Ohio River called for their aid.

There was little loss of life, and the destruction of property lay largely in the loss of stock and washing away of the soil, vegetation, and the means of production. Mr. Hiram Sibley, a noted seed dealer of Rochester, had become associated with the Red Cross and he put his religion into practice and gave $10,000 worth of seeds to replant the washed-out lands of the Mississippi.

Realizing that to be of any real service as a body of relief for sudden disasters, they formed a set of regulations which was as follows:

> 1. To never solicit relief or ask for contributions.
> 2. Not to pay salaries to officers—paying out money only to those whom we must employ for manual labor—and as our officers serve without compensation, they should not be taxed for dues.
> 3. To keep ourselves always in possession of a stated sum of money to commence a field of disaster—this sum to be independent even of the closed doors of a bank which might prevent leaving for a field on a Sunday or a holiday.
> 4. To take this sum of our own, going directly to a field with such help as needed, giving no notice until there, over-looking the field, and learning the extent of the trouble and conditions of the people, making immediate and reliable report to the country through the Associated Press, some of whose officers are our own Red Cross officers, as well. These reports would be truthful, unexaggerated, and non-sensational statements that could be relied upon.
> 5. That if, under these conditions, the people chose to make use of us as distributors of the relief which they desired to contribute to the sufferers, we would do our best to serve them while at the field—make report directly to each and all contributions, so far as in our power, and proceed to carry out any directions and apply the relief, at hand, in the wisest manner possible, among a dazed and afflicted community.

This provision has never for a day been broken and is as good today as it was in 1883.

In 1884, a fearful rise of the Ohio River causing great loss of life and property commanded their attention. Here they procured boats and launched out into the swollen torrent rescuing the people, after which they procured provisions and shelter for them. Before the close of the following year, 1885, came what was known as the Texas Famine. Thousands of miles of wild land, forming the Pan Handle, had been suddenly opened by the building of a Southern Railroad. And some thousands of families immigrated there. In just a few years, all they had was gone. Their crops could not grow on account of a drought. Starvation faced them. They could not leave the place; the rivers were dry from the Rio Grande to the Brazos. The cattle wandered here and there in the search for water and feed, and their bones whitened the plains. Who was more able to go to their relief than the Red Cross Society, which they did. And they shall ever be remembered by those people in deep love and appreciation.

In February 1888 occurred the Mount Vernon, Illinois, cyclone. In three minutes, the work of destruction was over. Ten minutes later, the sun shone out brightly. Fire broke out on every land, and the victims pinned down under the wreckage were subjects for the flames. The Red Cross Society arrived on this scene and did all in their power to relieve the suffering. During the same year, the yellow fever broke out in Jacksonville, Florida. The Red Cross sent no northern nurses, but eighteen or twenty "Howard nurses," mainly colored, went out from New Orleans under charge of Col. Fred F. Southmayd, their leader of twenty years in epidemics. And what a blessing these people going in His name, and under the auspices of the Red Cross Society proved to that fever-stricken district.

In May 1889, the Red Cross Society received word of the Johnstown flood. Here they labored, doing all in their power with God's help to relieve the suffering for five weary months. In the matter of sheltering the people, as in other of like importance, Miss Clara Barton, the president of the Association, was most helpful.

During the Russian famine of 1889–90, it was ascertained that Russia would gladly receive donations of relief from America and would send her ships for any food that might be offered. And when it was voted upon and defeated in the House, then the Red Cross, with the aid of the citizens of Washington, took up the matter. And what they did at this time, we all well know.

On the 28th of August 1893, a hurricane and tidal wave from the direction of the West Indies swept the coast of South Carolina, covering its entire range of Port Royal Islands sixteen feet below the sea. Some 4,000–5,000 perished and 30,000 remained with no earthly possession of home, clothing, or food. Here again, we see the Red Cross Society busy at work doing their utmost to relieve their conditions. They remained ten months.

Not long after their return they were asked to go to Turkey, where Armenian massacres were increasing quite rapidly. Besides the massacres in two cities of 10,000 people were down with four distinct epidemics. The report of the consuls had placed the number of deaths at one hundred per day. All this they entered and did their best. Their work was acceptable to Him who gave them the courage, protection, and strength to perform it, and they asked for nothing more.

In 1898, they are seen busy at work in Cuba at the time of oppression and the fight for liberty. We can see them here, there, anywhere they can lend a helping hand, and nursing the sick, wounded, and dying. In twenty-four hours, the surgeons had operated upon and dressed the wounds of 475 men. Four Red Cross sisters, all trained nurses, assisted the surgeons. Then yellow fever broke out in the camp. At first, just one case but it soon spread until there were 116 cases. Their work on that distressful field closed after nearly two years of hard toil, as one would never desire to repeat.

During the year 1900 at Galveston, the sea had overleaped its bounds and its victims by the thousands were in its grasp. Dead citizens lay by thousands amid the wreck of their homes, and raving maniacs searched the debris for their loved ones with the organized gangs of workers. Corpses were dumped by the barge loads into the Gulf. At least four thousand dwellings had been swept away with all their contents, and fully half of the population of the city was without shelter, food, clothes, or any of the necessaries of life. No description could adequately serve its purpose. But it was not long before the Red Cross clans commenced to gather. And what all they went through, God only knows.

The half can never be told of the splendid spirit shown by the citizens of the stricken San Francisco, when on the fateful 18th of April 1906, awakening to full realization of their common peril and misfortunes, foreshadowed by the ominous grotesqueness of ascending smoke-filled clouds, certain natural leaders of the bewildered multitude provided spontaneously for the temporary needs of the homeless. It was fortunate for San Francisco that the American National Red Cross Society had lately reorganized with special provisions in its charter that prepared it for just such an emergency as this greatest disaster of modern times. Within the stricken city were a number of devoted members of the local branch of that organization who, on the morning of the second day of horror, formed a nucleus of coherent and systematic workers that cared for the injured, provided food for the hungry, and shelter for the homeless. This philanthropic corporation was placed under government supervision, and William H. Taft, then Secretary of War, became its first president.

Problems of the most difficult nature confronted the Red Cross workers and their allies when they undertook the task of relieving three hundred thousand men, women, and children, bereft of homes and livelihood.

On the first of August, Dr. Devine retired from the Relief Commission, after more than three months of the most exacting work that has been required of any man in the nation. His time from seven in the morning until late at night was given without stint and without price, for it must be remembered that the services he rendered San Francisco were a free will offering of priceless value. His life work in relieving the unfortunate, and the Red Cross Society is only one of the altruistic organizations with which he is affiliated.

The half can never be told of the Red Cross's devotion to their duty and their high ideals. Thousands of persons have been helped to get on their feet after they had been stricken down by catastrophes of nature or operations of war.

> Is thy curse of comfort failing?
> Rise and share it with another.
> And through all the years of famine
> It shall serve thee and thy brother.
> Love divine will fill thy storehouse
> Or thy handful still renew;
> Scanty fare for one will, often,
> Make a royal feast for two.
>
> For the heart grows rich in giving;
> All its wealth is living grain;
> Seed which mildew in the garner,
> Scattered, fill with gold the plain.
> Is thy burden hard and heavy?
> Do thy steps drag wearily?
> Help to bear thy brother's burdens,
> God will bless both it and thee.
>
> Is the heart a well left empty?
> None but God its void can fill:
> Nothing but a ceaseless fountain
> Can its ceaseless longing still.
> Is the heart a living power?
> Self-entwined, its strength sinks low.
> It can only live in loving.
> And by serving, love will grow.
> (Mrs. Charles)

Charity gets its chief religious authority and incentive from Him who gave as the summary of all the law and prophets the coordinate commands to love God and to love our neighbor, and who, in explaining these commands, pronounced the parable of the Good Samaritan.

The **almshouse** is the fundamental institution in American poor relief. It cares for all the abjectly destitute not otherwise provided for. Its shelter is the guarantee against starvation which the State offers to all, no matter how unfortunate or degraded. But one of the sad things is, although this is God's work, for he said, "In as much as ye did it unto one of the least of these, my brethren, ye have done it unto me," no clergyman goes near the home the year round.

Besides the almshouses in giving relief to the poor, there is what is generally called **out-door relief**, that is, the relief of the poor in their own homes. This is one of the kindliest, and perhaps one of the cheapest, forms of relieving distress, and then only after a case has been found to belong to some special class requiring institutional care, should it be passed on to the limitations of institutional life. In this way the poor person is not separated from relatives and friends, families are not broken up, and the receipt of relief is not as conspicuous. Many families can almost support themselves and it seems folly to dismember them and place the children in refuges or board them in private families and compel the adults to go to the poor-house, when a little relief given in the house would keep the family together and enable them to make part of their support by ordinary methods.

In large centers of population, there are certain societies which, together with the churches and private individuals, do a considerable amount of relief work. Then there are a large number of dependent children left. In the United States alone there are 75,000. These are all cared for through charitable institutions. The numbers treated yearly in our hospitals who are unable to pay for treatment can hardly be estimated.

Standing between the religious orders of the Catholic Church and the paid nurses of the training schools are the orders of deaconesses of the Protestant denominations. The **Sisters of Charity** of the Catholic Church do "district nursing," which is simply nursing the sick poor in their homes, and they have attended to it with a devotion and an amount of personal sympathy that is hardly paralleled.

The **institution for the insane** should also be mentioned. One of the most pitiable sights I ever witnessed was while visiting the asylum here in Dayton—the poor pale faces, blank looks, mumbling talk, silly laughing, shrill shrieks. It is all as vivid to me as if it were yesterday. When Christ was here in person, he cast out the unclean spirits, but as his followers, we do the next best thing, caring for them, using wisdom in treatment and kindness in control until God in his infinite wisdom calls them home to Himself. Besides these institutions that have been named, there is an **asylum for the blind, deaf, and dumb**, which teaches the inmates to read and write.

All of these have been just alluded to under the heading of "Charities," while not done in the name of Christianity, but by the State. Still it is through the influence of Christianity that they have been brought about, insomuch as these institutions that care of the dependent ones is not heard of except where the gospel of Christ has been proclaimed.

One of the most beautiful examples of how a small thing that has the devotion of one pious and consecrated soul may grow to bless many nations is found in the career of Madame Garnier, the benevolent French widow who, some fifty years ago, founded the first **"House of Calvary"** in Lyons, France. Wishing to make her life a blessing to those whom others rather shunned, Madame Garnier ultimately settled upon poor women who were hopelessly sick with cancer. Her first two or three patients she took to her own home and there personally ministered to their every want until death relieved them. Like almost all things of this nature, at first it was up-hill work, and the Lyons House remained the only one for more than thirty years. After this, seven others followed.

A Mrs. Storr, while in Europe, read a notice in the entrance of one of the churches that upon a certain Sunday a sermon would be preached by a priest well-known for his eloquent fervor about the work of the House of Calvary. That was the first Mrs. Storrs had ever heard of the work. She made inquiries and the result was that she studied the work for a few years, then on arriving home, she started the noble work here in America. The work did not succeed in a day, for it was five years before the gilt sign "House of Calvary" was put up over the door of No. 5 Perry Street, New York. Although under the control of the Catholic women, the House of Calvary, in so far as the reception and care of patients is concerned, is absolutely non-sectarian. Protestants, Hebrews, all are welcome—all just as kindly cared for. Patients who can afford to pay, even a small sum, are not received; the aim of the ladies who are at the head of this work being to furnish a home, not a hospital, for those who are sick, and poor, and homeless.

There are 101 churches in Buffalo, of all denominations, that have accepted small districts from the **Charity Organization Society**, within which they agree to be responsible for the care of neglected poor of any faith. The plan began in 1896 with sixty-six churches. It can be almost said that every church in Buffalo now has a district under this plan.

The higher side of the plan consists not in the giving out of alms and supplies, but in the development among those who take a district of such a spirit of loving friendliness and neighborliness as will make them seek to know, as well as to help, those who live within the neighborhood in their charge.

Those who are at work in modern charity need continually to refresh their minds with the thought of the real spirit that is behind them and of which this work is one of the modern expressions. With every such institution as the Associated Charities there ought to be a great, enthusiastic, sympathetic public. They are simply trying to do on a large scale what some of us are trying to do on a small scale when now and then we really grapple with the cause of need. They are trying to do for society what we are trying to do for one or two persons here and there. And this little army of friendly visitors is composed of persons who, with absolute devotion and seeking nothing for themselves in return, are just giving themselves, out of human love, to the service of those who are in need, and they are trying to do that work, not now and then, but all the time.

Among philanthropic societies, the **Young Men's Christian Association** has high standing; but it is more than a philanthropic society. Behind all its philanthropic work, and giving power to it, is a persistent religious motive; but the Association is more than a religious society. It has set forth a vigorous and wholesome practical type of Christianity—indeed, more than any other organization, it has presented Christianity to the world, not merely as a method of rescue from some present or future disaster, but also as a mode of positive and even exuberant living; but the Association is more than a Christian Society. It is an arm, an instrument, of the Church. On the contrary, whatever it has done, the Church has done. The Church has provided the motive power; the Association has provided the mechanism.

And now just a word concerning **Settlements** or settlement work. They are the schools or entering wedges of that democracy which God is building up in the evolution of civilization. What the Settlement does attempt to do is to communicate, to make common property in the best things of life—things that would make any life larger, any spirit more perfect. The Settlement is a station for investigation of actual conditions and already has proved useful in this field.

The Hartford Settlement, in cooperation with the "Committee of Fifty," makes a local study of the liquor traffic, drinking habits and customs, and their effects on the people. Residents of Kingsley House have given attention to foods dietaries. Tenement houses have been studied by nearly all the Settlements. Settlements have sought to mitigate the evils of crowded homes by sending the feeble and convalescent to the country for recuperation. Trained nurses are valuable allies. These, the Settlement furnishes. Working people are worn out with toil and often lack skill. At these times, to be able to command the attention of a trained nurse several times a day often makes all the difference between life and death. Direct relief agencies can go a very little way to aid the poor. But charity has its place in a method of economic help.

For the present, the very existence of many thousands of persons depends on the gifts of those who are more fortunate. There will always be some who will be too weak to provide for their own necessities. The Settlement acts as any gentle and kind household must act in presence of extreme destitution; it must give material help. There are plenty of people to preach thrift and advise economy. But the Settlements provide conveniences for saving. It promotes educational interests, directly and indirectly, by furnishing instruction, and by agitation, and administration with the purpose of improving the public system. It seeks to cultivate the spirit of friendship, because it is itself an element of welfare and happiness.

The value of the fundamental settlement idea, that of identification of its life with that of the neighborhood, had in the course of time to appeal not only to the individuals, but also to already ensuing social forces.

Charitable societies and especially churches saw the advantage that settlements obtained in being always on the ground and in the establishment of nearer relationship to facts and people than others enjoyed.

Societies and churches hence began to adopt the plan of establishing settlements as agents, frontier posts for charitable or religious work, thus instituting a new sort of mission. We cannot fail to notice that the settlements have in their experimentation proved the value of various forms of social improvement which in turn have often been set on their own feet or have been taken over by other agencies.

Especially has the growth of municipal activity been very marked during this period. In the larger cities, therefore, one activity after another that the settlement has developed has been taken over by the city itself, as in the case of manual training, kindergartens, playgrounds, domestic training, etc. The function of the public school has been greatly enlarged. The departments of health and of parks have recognized claims hitherto not felt.

A social movement of interest beyond mere denominational lines has recently been inaugurated by a number of **Methodist** laymen and clergymen. But the movement is by no means foreign to the genius of Methodism, for the original Holy Club at Oxford University, out of which Methodism grew, gave itself from the beginning to work among the sick and the imprisoned. J. R. Green, in his *History of the English People*, says "The noblest result of the Methodist revival was the steady attempt which has never ceased from that day to this, to remedy the guilt, the ignorance, the physical suffering, the social degradation of the profligate and the poor."

John Wesley started a poor man's bank, a poor man's lawyer, a poor man's doctor, a labor factory for the unemployed, a household salvage corps, a prison mission, the first cheap printing press, free public libraries, and even associated charities. And what this church has done, all evangelical denominations have done.

In its true spirit all settlement work is essentially religious. With this conclusion some may disagree, but in fact, it is so. From a small beginning the settlement house now cares for a thousand boys and girls, and young men and women, who find their common playground, the only social opportunities many of them know; and tired mothers, a blessed respite from the cares of their hard life. These are the things that appeal to the eye, a teeming hive in which clubs, classes, social meetings, gymnasiums, games, kindergartens, and like activities go on unceasingly.

Miss **Helen Gould** upon the death of her father in 1892, fell heir to a large fortune, which she has since expended liberally in a large variety of benevolent activities. Her life history, in fact, is largely a record of philanthropic deeds. In 1898, at the time of the Spanish war, she gave one hundred thousand dollars to the United States government. She also contributed liberally to the work of the Woman's National War Relief Association. She donated twenty-five thousand dollars for supplies for the relief camp of sick, wounded, and convalescent soldiers. The full extent of Miss Gould's charities will never be known to anyone but herself.

One of her first charities was the establishment at Woodycrest, a charming old colonial place near her own country home at Irvington on the Hudson, a haven for crippled children picked up in the slums. Summer and winter, a number of blanched little folk with deformed bodies are nursed there to health and happiness. It is no stinted charity that mothers these lucky waifs. A mansion is their home, and sloping lawns over-run with wild flowers, and fanned by the breezes of the Hudson are their playground.

Her income is approximately a million dollars a year or nearly three thousand dollars a day, but of this scarcely more than a tenth is expended on its owner. The rest she regards as a sort of trust for the less fortunate.

A prominent preacher of half a century ago was asked by an unbeliever if he did not think that after all the Christian religion were a failure. He replied, "We don't know, it never has been tried." But there died in New York, a short time ago, a man named Samuel H. Hadley who "tried" the Christian religion after the manner of its Founder—really tried it; and it worked. He kept a resort on Water Street for those fallen wretches whom he frankly called "bums." When they lied to him and stole the very dishes on which he gave them food, as they often did, he ignored their thefts; and when they smirkingly confessed themselves "saved" for the sake of a warm bed, he asked no questions, but honestly rejoiced till they were shamed into a confession and a new start. There was no limit to his patience; he called it "love." By "loving" a man long enough and sincerely enough, you can win him that's the whole thing. But except in very, very rare cases, this "love," as we practice it and call it religion, gives out long before it reaches the winning point.

Hadley's "greatness" consisted in the fact that his "love" never gave out. Social workers and ministers came from all over the country and from other countries, and were sent by all denominations to inquire into the "methods" of so successful a mission. But the methods were too simple to allure. Visitors saw merely a few Bible texts such as they had been brought up on, the same that are hung on the walls of every Sunday school. Many earnest workers went away only half satisfied; no panacea had been discovered after all. There was no solution of the great problem, they saw only a reformed drunkard and "bum" helping other drunkards and bums. But he was a man of such a shining personality that other men came to him naturally and eagerly. Then he practiced the forgiveness of his brother unto seventy times seven. That was all, a single spark of Christ's own fire, and the Bible for his manual.

There will never be known just what number of "cases" could be marked "cured" by the Water Street Mission. But this fact we do know. A really large number of men are today self-respecting persons who went there sots; that many of them hold places of respect and influence; and that much hot coffee and strong meat stew were daily given to those who would surely go into the depths again to come back heavy with liquor and crime. It was given as freely to them as to anybody else. When many of them turned and scoffed him for being a fool to feed them and believe in them, this man still worked on, and in his quaint revivalist phraseology "sowed seeds of grace." But he won and saved men as who else does? The last words that he uttered were "Who will care for my poor bums?" [Taken from *The World's Work: A History of our Time* by Walter Hines Page and Arthur Wilson Page, 1905.]

Mr. Hadley, while others had been talking, he had been doing. No man of his day has done more, if as much, to reach the hopeless victims of sinful habits, to lift them out of the horrible pit and miry clay and set their feet upon a rock and put into their mouth a new song.

Mr. Hadley loved all and gave all. His own comfort was nothing. His passion for souls was a consuming fire. He rejoiced to suffer with and for those he sought to save. In his mission, the hungry found bread; the naked clothing; the weak, a strong arm, and the hopeless, inspiration. He did not give what cost him nothing. He starved himself to feed and he robbed himself to provide.

Most of us are common place Christians. Our range is on the earth. Now, what can be expected of ordinary, commonplace Christians? Of those who understand daily duties, but have no special enthusiasm, whose life is taken up with life's ordinary duties, and who have no time and no aptitude for unusual revelations, and no particular consciousness of an immortal God? For them, there is possible the substantial essence of religion, which does not consist of deep experiences, but in duty performed. They cannot give much time to special religious meditation or prayer, but a great deal to their daily service for their fellowmen honestly, truly, patiently, lovingly performed. They are the kind described in one of the Psalms as those who shalt abide in the Lord's tabernacle because they walk uprightly, speak truth, slander not, despise an evil man, and keep their oaths; who, as a prophet says, do justly, show mercy, and walk humbly before God, they possess religion because they are tender to the fatherless and the widow and keep themselves spotless in an evil world. These are attainments, within reach of all, attained by multitudes of people who practice these virtues in their homes, in their daily work and business, in the narrow circle of their acquaintances. If they are not praying all the time, or thinking of God, they are doing better, because they are doing their duty as it lies next to them.

The religion of the future will be the religion of brotherhood. In the mind of every thoughtful man, there stands out as never before the one ideal of this religion, the Man of Sorrows, he who said, "Thou shalt love the Lord thy God with all thy heart, soul, and mind, and thou shalt love thy neighbor as thyself."

Salvation
Maud E. Hoyle

(This is the earliest known sermon of Maud's, delivered on February 20, 1910, at the Lagonda Avenue United Brethren Church, Springfield, Ohio.)

Text: "Whosoever shall call upon the name of the Lord shall be saved." (Romans 10:13)

Friends, I want to talk to you tonight of salvation. Is there a need of salvation? If there is, why are we as Christians, ones who have been saved by this great salvation by calling upon the name of the Lord, not more energetic and awake bringing others to Him?

I asked this question the other evening, if there was a need of salvation. The parties that I was with thought it a ridiculous question, saying, "Why, what a question—of course there is." I said, "Well, why is there?" One replied, "Why, because if there was no salvation, we would not go to heaven when we die." And that was the only answer I could get.

Friends, you may enumerate and think out for yourselves why there is a need of salvation. But do not, I pray you, have all of your answers be subjective. It is proper and indispensable to call upon Him because:

1. We have sinned against God, and it is right that we should confess it.

2. Because He only can pardon us, and it is fit, that if we obtain pardon, we should ask it of God.

3. And to call upon Him is to acknowledge Him as our Sovereign, our Father, and our Friend; and it is right that we render Him our homage.

We hear a great deal today of "Why can't we have an old-time revival again?" And to hear some talk, one would think that God had withdrawn His guiding hand, when in reality, it all lay with the people.

Friends, if we want an old-time revival, we will have to get it in the old-time way. The promise is the same today as it was years, yes, centuries ago. "Whosoever shall call upon the name of the Lord shall be saved."

The deep sense of sin explains in large measure the lack of spiritual earnestness and of spiritual power. If you have noticed, every great spiritual awakening has had as a necessary element a deepening sense of sin. I can think of no truer test as to whether we are growing in spirituality than this. Are we becoming increasingly sensitive to the approaches of sin? Does the sinfulness of sin continue to grow upon us? Are we becoming increasingly haters of sin? The *Westminster Confession of Faith* says that sin is "any transgression or want of conformity with the law of God." It embraces sins of omission, as well as sins of commission. Sin is everywhere prevalent. With whom among us does it not linger in some form, to some degree? If any one doubts this, let him remember the warning of St. John, "If we say we have no sin, we deceive ourselves and the truth is not in us." The person does not live who does not at times fall short from the highest requirements of a holy God.

The problem of life is a large one in which we are intensely interested. Each of us is seeking to solve it in the best way, though we make many blunders in our attempts to do so. In this connection, we are ever seeking and giving help, and we realize the constant need of it. The houses in which we live, the food we eat, the fuel and light we burn, the clothes we wear, all tell of needs. Think to what extent we are dependent upon one another for help. Our schools, stores, factories, and farms are proof of this. The supply of these needs means life to us. And whatever is helpful is, to that extent, a savior.

Besides the body's needs, we have mental ones, and upon these depends the mind's ability to care well for the body. If the body be neglected and sickens, it reacts and causes the mind trouble. But though we have found abundant supply for bodily wants, and have stored our minds with knowledge, we may yet feel unsatisfied. Among sick and poor, learned and unlearned, you will find those who are wretched and unhappy because of other wants that are not supplied. These wants have to do with the heart. The mind is fretful, and the face worn because of heart unrest. Only as this is satisfied can the body and mind be at their best. By interesting the mind in something absorbing, you may forget for a time the heart's needs, and so the harm continues without your being conscious of it. In vain efforts to change your condition, you may become discouraged and give up altogether.

Often people think that their bodily needs, circumstances and surroundings are to blame for this unhappiness, and so they expend much of their time and thought in seeking to better these. As they are changed such persons may seem happy for the moment, but they soon feel unsatisfied again. Living in this state is living in sin as the Bible terms it, and the final end of which is heart destruction, or death. It is from such a state and its ends that the Bible teaches God would save us. Sin is of such a character that while at first, it is detestable, it comes to be regarded as extremely pleasing, and in time, as absolutely necessary. And so, the word of warning, "Be not deceived," spoken in connection with the working of sin, is a timely word, and reveals a knowledge of a deceiving power. In the West Indies, there is a kind of a bat which sucks the blood of its victims while they are asleep. It is said that it will fan its victim into deeper sleep while it goes on drawing life. In the same manner, sin will deceive while it carries on its work of ruin.

But no sin can be concealed from God. He sees us through and through. There is nothing hidden from

Him. He judges us, not by the exterior, but by the heart. He understands our motives in life, the hidden recesses of the heart. And then, too, not so many of our sins are hidden from other people as we think. One's face reveals more concerning his thoughts than he realizes. Sin tolerated in one's life is like the white ants of Africa that gnaw out the inside of a piece of furniture, leaving the outside uninjured, until some day, it crumbles at just a touch.

It goes without any argument that sin separates one from the best in his own day and generation. They lose interest in the good and the best. Sin breaks up even the strongest human tie we know, that of natural affection. Every person knows of some families that have been slivered and torn asunder by sin.

A number of years ago, a man belonged to this church who fell through the temptation of strong drink. He sold his shoes, coat, and even his Bible to gratify the appetite. The church sought him, his mother pleaded with him, his brothers and sisters tried to win him back, but it was of no use. He was lost to church, home, and friends. What did it? I know of nothing else that does this but sin. It separates chief friends; it destroys families; it slivers the social structure. And above all, do not forget that it alienates men from God now.

There can be no doubt about it. The most serious thing is that sin ultimately leads to that awful condemnation of Jesus Christ. You remember the words "Depart from Me." Oh, the loneliness of the life of sin. It plunges a man into gloom which ever deepens in this life, and at last, casts him into utter darkness. Then, have you ever noticed how enslaving sin is? The Bible states that he "that committeth sin is the servant, or slave of sin." We begin with just some trifle – telling a little story, playing marbles for keeps, playing cards for a premium, taking a social glass, going to a little family dance. In a little while, if we are not careful, we will become gamblers, drunkards, and frequent the public dance hall. When you speak to one on this matter, he will probably tell you, "I mean to keep sin my captive. I am not going to yield to this thing to such an extent that it grips me." But if you will notice, it will wind closer and closer; it will tighten its grip; it will gather in momentum. Sin is slavery. "If any man committeth sin, he is the servant of sin." God pity the one among us who feels the galling fetters sinking into his life.

Sin also has exhausting power. An act of sin, as a rule, does not stand still or alone. It multiplies. If you entertain a wrong thought once, it becomes easier to think it the second time, and how much easier after we have thought it a few score of times. Sin does not stop with one part of one's being. Body, mind, and spirit are one. Sin spreads like leaven until it leavens the whole lump.

Now as to our influence, shall it be for good or for evil? For good—then let no act of ours be such as could lead a fellow mortal astray. It is a terrible thought that some careless word uttered, even if said in jest, may start some soul upon the downward road. Oh, it is terrible power that we have—the power of influence, and it clings to us. We cannot shake it off. It speaks, it walks, it moves. It is powerful in every look of our eye, in every word, in every act of our lives. We cannot live to ourselves. We must be either a light to illumine, or a tempest to destroy. We must bear constantly in mind that there is one record we cannot interline, our lives written on another's heart. How gladly we would review and write a kind word there, a generous act here, erase a frown, and put in a loving word, a bright smile. Harshness would be erased, and gentleness written. But not so. What is written is written.

The clock in a jeweler's window fronting on the main street of a little Western town, stopped and for half an hour, the hands pointed to a quarter of nine. It seemed a trifling thing, but a surprising amount of confusion resulted from that temporary lapse. Children saw the clock indicating that they had fifteen minutes to spare and stopped to play until the warning note of the distant school bell told them of their misplaced confidence. A business man, after a glance at the clock, took his walk to the station in a more leisurely manner than he had planned, and missed his train in consequence. People were late to their offices and late in keeping appointments, all because a clock had stopped. And the strange thing was that not one of them had realized how much he was relying upon that timekeeper until its departure from correctness had led him astray. Sometimes we feel that we exert no influence over those about us. And yet, we may be sure, insignificant and uninfluential as we seem, our lives are either leading souls to God or away from God.

There was a certain thistle introduced into New York. Large sums of money have been expended to stop its spreading, but in vain. It has spread until it is all over that state and into other states. So, it is with sin, no one can measure its propagating power. No one can tell how far its influence will reach. God only knows that.

This brings me to the consequences of sin. When sin has grown and grown until it is fully grown, it bringeth forth death. In this life, it undermines the physical life. It blights the intellectual nature. It makes absolutely impossible the highest achievement in one's life work. It slowly kills conscience until its voice becomes more and more husky and indistinct.

And in the life to come, we will be castaways, with no fellowship with the Father, though we should seek for it diligently with tears. Do you wonder that tonight I entreat that every one of us hate sin with a deadly hatred? That I entreat that every one of us declare warfare against sin until we die? That I entreat that we do not tolerate even little sins in our lives, that we give no place to sin?

Now, if we are saved from the guilt of sin, from the power of sin, from the condemnation of sin, from the consequences of sin, in this life and the life to come, by calling upon the name of the Lord, we will be saved to, and have peace with, God. Oh, what a blessing it is to be at peace or to have a reconciliation with God. Oh, if we could only realize the wonderous truth that the blessed Saviour left heaven to seek and save on earth those who not only did not seek Him but who were at enmity to Him. It will also save us to access God for all our needs. He says, "If ye abide in me, and my words abide in you, ask whatsoever ye will, and it shall be done unto you."

Then, too, it saves us to the ageless life here and hereafter. And this is the record that God hath given to us eternal life, and this life is in his Son. Of all things in the universe, this is the great prize we should seek with all our hearts and souls, for it includes every other good—God, heaven, holiness, usefulness, happiness. Just so far as we have eternal life can we know God or heaven, or the highest good.

Therefore, like Bunyan's Pilgrim, fleeing from the city of Destruction with his fingers on his ears, crying out "Life, Life," so we should run from the city of Spiritual Death to the city of Eternal Life. It is not a salvation that concerns the future alone or benefits us then only. It is, as the present is, saved that the future is made larger. Sin is what hurts, yet we are apt to get the idea that God saves *in* sin rather than *from* it. What you are when saved should mean much more than what you were at the beginning. You began life like the baby oak just bursting from the acorn. As you grow into the light and life of companionship with God, you may unfold and develop perfectly.

Salvation is made possible on the easiest terms. Just call upon the name of the Lord. I wish you would try to imagine how the people who knew Jesus best at the time He was here in the body must have learned to love Him. He not only told them wonderful secrets respecting life, which caused them to think life worth living, but He lived this life before them—a life the grandest and loveliest, though very different from theirs. But it was not for His life alone that they loved Him, but for Himself. He was ever thinking of them. He was ready to add to their comfort at any cost to Himself. Though they called Him "Master," He was one among them as one that served. How could they help loving Him with a love stronger than death?

At one time, when He was going upon a dangerous journey, His disciples said, "Let us go also and die with Him." At length, He began to talk to them of being crucified and parting from them. Upon hearing this, they were in deep sorrow, until He unfolded to them His plan of returning in spirit, and so of being ever with them. This came about. He returned in spirit. Most wonderful happiness followed, and it was now that they began to tell others of Him.

It was on one of the first of these occasions that Peter said, "Neither is there salvation in any other for there is no other name under heaven given among men whereby we must be saved." He spake of something which the disciples all knew, for in Jesus they felt that they had found everything.

We have too small and mean an estimate of what is included in salvation. It is not only saving the germ that now is, but the never-fading flower that should grow from each life. It is not so much what we are saved *from* as from what we are saved *to*—that is, to the countless ages of glory. God has planned an eternal kingdom for each.

Hear Jesus say, "Come ye blessed of my Father, inherit the kingdom, prepared for you from the foundation of the world," call upon the name of the Lord. It is implied in this, that we call upon Him with right feelings—that is with a humble sense of our sinfulness, and our need of pardon, and with a willingness to receive eternal life as it is offered in the Bible. And if this be done, this passage teaches us that salvation is possible to everyone. He will cast none away who come in this manner. The invitation is extended to all. Salvation is certain, for God says it. And the word of the Lord abideth forever. The Lord will not call back His word. Our God is a covenant-keeping God.

We have then only to ascertain what Christ hath spoken to us concerning our salvation, and to believe His word in order to enjoy forgiveness, and to rejoice in hope of eternal life. There are thousands of promises which Christ hath spoken, and we may safely take Him at any one of them. "Whosoever calleth upon the name of God shall be saved." "Him that cometh unto me, I will in no wise cast out." All we have to do is to put these invitations to the test. Salvation is certain because Jesus provides it. The Redeemer is provided in the person of the Messiah of the prophecy, but this redemption is secured only through the death of Jesus, and it must be complied with by a personal acceptance. He speaks to you from the bloody cross—come, just come, come just as you are, and He will give you pardon for the past, and grace for the future. He himself has made all the sacrifice necessary, and He has done it so completely that there is nothing whatever left for you to do, but just to come.

The Holy Spirit supplies it. When we turn away from our sins with our honest heart and trust not in our own poor works, but in Jesus Christ as our sin-bearer and Saviour, then the Holy Spirit will give us that peace we find in our hearts which is born alone of that Spirit whom "If any man have not, he is not of his." The Spirit beareth witness with our spirit that we are the children of God.

Then again, the experience of thousands affirm it. Don't you want to be among the number that are on the Lord's side? Is there any here tonight in whose lives are hidden sins that have not been reckoned with? Draw near to Jesus Christ, the great Saviour from sins. He only can cancel the stains caused by past wrongdoings. Let us be thorough in this. If we have sin and will confess our sins to Christ, He is faithful and just to forgive us our sins and to cleanse us from all unrighteousness. Let us not only confess our sins, but forsake it, forever. If we have wronged another, let us make it right. Is there one here that wants cleansing? He will cleanse you. Let Him take such possession of you that you can say, "It is not I that liveth, but Christ liveth in me." It is only Divine power that can break these bonds of sin. Come, whosoever will let Him, call upon the name of the Lord and be saved.

Two Gardens
Maud E. Hoyle

(While no date was noted on this sermon, it was in the same notebook as Maud's first sermon given at the Lagonda Avenue United Brethren Church in 1910. It is likely from the same time period.)

Text: "And Jehovah God planted a garden eastward in Eden; and there he put the man whom he had formed." (Gen 2:8) and

"Now in the place where he was crucified there was a garden; and in the garden a new sepulcher, wherein was never man yet laid." (John 19:41)

Friends, it is no new story but the same old story I bring to you tonight, of sin and redemption, failure and victory. I have chosen as a theme "Two Gardens." The first is the garden of man's fall. The text is found in Genesis 2, verse 8. "And Jehovah God planted a garden eastward in Eden; and there he put the man whom he had formed." The location of Eden is unknown beyond the fact that it includes at least portions of the Euphrates and Tigris. We have no definite knowledge, nor do we know the extent of the district or province of Eden in which this garden was situated. But the location is not so much what we are interested in tonight, as what makes it stand out so bold in history.

This garden was a park, a pleasure garden. It contained the most beautiful trees, streams, flowers, and fruits. But the greatest charm of the garden was the "Tree of Life" (which was probably not a single tree but a species of tree) and another most wonderful and attractive tree, the "Tree of Knowledge of Good and Evil." It was a wonderful garden, a true garden of God.

In this garden, Adam and Eve dwelt for a time with a wide range to their life and enjoyment in the variety and beauty and flavor of the fruits, the loveliness of nature, and above all, the blessedness of communion with God. But it proved to be but a temporary nursery for the human family; thence men, had they remained innocent, would have spread out in every direction until the whole earth became the "Garden of the Lord." God's purpose, though deferred, will in His own time be realized by the Second Adam, the Lord of heaven. Every step in this garden story is our story. The child Adam is our looking glass.

Let us look for awhile at man in his Eden home. He was innocent, but not a savage, except in outward surroundings and appliances. Victor Hugo's awful picture of a man in the ocean with the vast and silent heavens above, the desolate waves around, the birds like dwellers in another world circling in the evening light, and the poor fellow trying to swim he knows not where, is the picture of what the first man would be, alone and without direct help from God. But Adam had companionship and help.

The Tree of Life like that in the city of God was doubtless medical. The tree of Knowledge of Good and Evil was not the "tree of knowledge," but only of the knowledge of good and evil. It was not there to make them fall into sin, but to train them in virtue by resisting temptation. It was necessary that there should be something forbidden that seemed desirable. There was no other way of opening the door to man's highest possibility, his fullest development, his pure holiness, his greatest happiness, his largest usefulness.

All who would become strong and useful must gain their power largely through victory over temptation.

Whether this was a real or a symbolic tree is of little account, though it is impossible to conceive of a more simple and natural test of obedience than such a forbidden tree when we remember that Adam was but a child in development. It is like the forbidden objects by which we train children. It is true that human life is a restricted life, a life subjected to law; and he who confesses this subjection remains in Eden; and he who denies it is banished.

The forbidden tree stands in every paradise of virtue and enjoyment. God has made a boundless provision for natural appetites, but there is always a limit, in going beyond which paradise is lost. The desire of progress, of acquiring property, of enjoying earth's blessing, is right; but the forbidden tree of gaining them by injuring others, by falsehood, or fraud or selfishness, stands near. God wants us to enjoy, but in the heavenly way. This man, though placed in most desirable surroundings and having the pleasant work of caring for this beautiful garden, the tempter came one day. "Yea, hath God said, Ye shall not eat of any tree of the garden? God is very good, but has He not laid some useless and trying restrictions upon you? Surely, these must be a mistake. If he loved you, could he shut you away from the delicious fruit on yonder tree? Are you to live in paradise and not be able to enjoy it?"

See how Satan persistently points to the few restrictions and not to the wide range of privileges? Millions of trees and countless varieties of fruits were free, but they were led to dwell on the one forbidden thing. This is still a specimen of his tactics. Eve replies, "We may eat of all, except one," laying emphasis on the liberality of God's gifts and on the danger of disobeying. But at the same time, she left out three emphatic expressions in her quotation of God's permission—"every tree," "freely," and "surely die"—which shows that the temptation was beginning to take effect. Whoever parleys with temptation today is already on the verge of danger. We all know the remainder of this story. Enough has been said to see the tragedy of sin—the tragedy of the universe. *Would* we have done better than Adam and Eve? We can tell most easily by answering the question, "*Have* we done better?"

Now to mention a few of the consequences of sin. They became ashamed, self-conscious; they were afraid of their heavenly Father. Sin makes cowards of us all. It brought injury to others. While each one of us makes our own choices as really as Adam did, yet, Adam's sin brought unfavorable inherited tendencies and environment. Sin brought death. We must not think by this that if man had not sinned his body would not have passed away, that death would not have been. No, not that, but death by sin became death, otherwise it would have been only a transition to a higher sphere as is suggested by the translation of Enoch, Moses, and Elijah, and the transformation of the body at the resurrection. "The sting of death is sin." They were banished from their Eden home. And the last consequence is perpetual conflict, a warfare not yet ended, but is raging as intensely as ever. But there is also a promise here, a prediction of a time when man will conquer his great enemy, sin.

So, turning from the child man in his garden home, who yielded to temptation, and the vision of the long line of evils such yielding has brought, let us turn our attention to the second garden, the garden of man's recovery. Try to catch a vision of Christ, who was tempted like as we are, but gained the victory. He showed us the way and gives us the help by which we, too, may gain the victory. This second garden is the garden in which Christ was crucified. For as in Adam all die, so also in Christ shall all be made alive.

"Now in the place where He was crucified there was a garden." (John 19:41). The world has seen many fearful scenes, such as the horrors of the siege of Jerusalem, of the Black Hole of Calcutta, of the London plague, of Indian massacres, of the Chicago fire, of the San Francisco earthquake. It has witnessed many heroic scenes. But in all history no tragedy is so black, no scene so heroic, as that which occurred in this garden. It is that darkest part of night which comes just before the dawn. Jesus, after His last talk with His disciples, crossed the brook Kedron, taking with Him only Peter, James, and John to be eye-witnesses to the church of his agony and afford Him their sympathy. He advanced from the moonlit part into the deep shade. Shrinking from contact with Satan, sin, and death, He knelt and fell forward on the earth, a stone's cast distance from the disciples, praying, "My Father, if it be possible, let this cup pass away from me, never the less, not as I will, but as thou wilt."

His using that imparted physical strength, only to agonize in prayer, even to bloody sweat falling as drops to the ground. Three times, Jesus returned to the slumbering apostles, each time to find them asleep, and so having lost the precious opportunity which afterwards they would look back on with bitter regret. As it was, He endured the conflict bereft of human sympathy and alone.

Already as Christ was uttering His sad words of disappointment to the disciples of "Sleep on now," the lantern and torches of His captors were gleaming through the trees. A band from the Roman cohort came down under the guidance of the priests by party's officers, elders, captains of the temple, chief priests, and Judas. Jesus in calm dignity came forth to meet them. The traitor gave his studied kiss. Jesus asks, "Whom seek ye?" This question was asked for the purpose of shielding his disciples, by drawing the attention of all upon Himself.

The disciples all fled, but John and Peter soon returned. Jesus was bound and led for a private, informal examination before Annas. Afterward, He was taken before Caiaphas, where He was condemned for blasphemy. Night trials being illegal at dawn, He was formally condemned before the Sanhedrin, and taken to Pilate, the accusation being changed to sedition. Pilate declares Him innocent, but sends Him to Herod, who returns him as harmless. Pilate again and again tried to release Him, but at the clamor of the Jews, he delivered Jesus to the soldiers to be scourged and mocked. They placed a crown of thorns upon His head and clothed Him in a purple robe. Soon the sad procession moved out of the castle. In advance was a soldier carrying a white wooden board on which was written the nature of the crime. Next came four soldiers, under a centurion, with the hammer and the nails, guarding Jesus, who bore, as always in such cases, the cross on which He was to suffer. Then came two robbers, each bearing his cross and guarded by four more soldiers.

As they went forth into the street, they were followed by a great multitude. But just before they reached the garden wherein He is crucified, and probably just outside of the Damascus gate, Jesus, weak and weary from his sufferings, was unable to bear the weight of the cross. A man named Simon, from Cyrene in northern Africa, meeting the procession, was compelled to help Jesus bear His cross. The after part of the cross (the lighter part), which usually dragged upon the ground, was put upon Simon. Simon was a picture of every Christian. But here, as always, the Saviour bears the heaviest part of the burden, while the lightest part rests on the one who follows after him.

It was the kindly custom of Jewish ladies to give to those who were being crucified a stupefying draught of wine, mingled with a powerful narcotic drug. It was bitter but was offered as an anesthetic to stupefy and dull the senses of pain. Jesus recognized this beautiful act of kindness by tasting the draught, but He was true to His mission and His work of redemption by refusing to drink it. He would drink the cup of suffering for the sin of the world. As God's will was shown at Gethsemane in not taking away the cup, He prayed that He need not drink, so He would not Himself, against the will of God, take away that cup by stupefying His sense of suffering.

Jesus was nailed to the cross while it was lying on the ground, then it was slowly raised with the sufferer upon it. The feet of the sufferer were only a foot or two above the ground. Crucifixion was an unspeakable, awful form of death. It was the most cruel and shameful of all punishments. But the most revolting feature of death by this method was that the torture was deliberately prolonged. For five hours, Jesus endured this pain of torn nerves and intense thirst and racked body, and throbbing brain. The two robbers were crucified, the one on the right hand, and the other on the left, in order to give the impression that Jesus was also a malefactor. But in the spiritual, this had another meaning. "He was numbered with the transgressors" in order that He might show His sympathy with them, that He might reach their hearts and lead them to a better life.

We may well believe that all the words of our Lord as He hung upon the cross have been preserved. John was there, with quick ear. The three Marys were there—Mary, the mother of Jesus, Mary, the wife of Clopas; and Mary Magdalene. Many other women were there, and doubtless the other disciples. Many scoffers also were there who also would catch up Christ's words but in a different spirit.

In a very wonderful way, the seven utterances that have come down to us represent the seven most important phases of Christ's character and work. The first word was a word of **forgiveness** which was probably spoken as the cross was planted in the ground, with a rough shock of indescribable agony. "Father, forgive them for they know not what they do." His coming to earth was to prove God's readiness to forgive men and this includes even His murderers, the harsh soldiers, Annas, Caiaphas, Herod, Pilate, and, us, too, when by our sins we crucify the Son of God afresh.

The second word was a word of **salvation**. One of the robbers moved by Christ's tender words of forgiveness and probably having heard of Him before, he rebukes the other robber and begs for Christ to help him. Jesus answers, "Today shalt thou be with me in paradise." How quickly does Christ respond. He came for that purpose to seek and save the lost.

His third word was a word of **love**. Jesus probably had the care of His mother and at this time looking toward John He says, "Woman, behold thy son," and then looking at His mother says to John, "Behold thy mother." And from that hour, the disciple took her into his own home.

The fourth word was a word of **atonement**. It was spoken toward the close of that mysterious darkness that seized the country from noon until three o'clock, when the Son of God felt as if He had been deserted by His Father. "My God, my God, why hath thou forsaken me?" It was a feeling, not a fact. This cry was the expression of a human experience in many an hour of darkness and despair, without which Jesus would not have been in all points tempted like as we are, yet without sin.

The fifth word was a word of **physical suffering**. Only when all else had been attended to was Christ free to attend to His own physical sensations. "I thirst." It is His sole expression of bodily suffering. This pain, as in the case of wounded soldiers, swallowed up all other agonies. They fill a sponge and put it around a stalk of hyssop, and thus applied the restorative to His mouth.

The sixth work is a word of **triumph**. He had reached the climax of suffering and His work was done. "It is finished," He cried aloud. What was finished? His life's work, the cup of suffering, the atonement for the sins of the world, the old era and dispensation. In one sense nothing He did was ended. But the atoning sacrifice had been offered once for all.

Then in lower tones, He added the seventh word which was a word of **reunion**. "Father, into thy hands I commend my spirit." There was a moment of stillness and then a piercing shriek rent the air, and His head fell upon His breast. He was dead. He gave Himself for our sins.

The tendency of today, especially among the young, is to speak of sin lightly. But the crucifixion emphasizes the fact that sin is a deicide—that it killed the Son of God. If sin caused all of this agony to Jesus, should we look upon it with the least degree of allowance?

And this is the record, that God hath given to us eternal life, and this life is in His son. But many of us are living today as if we were our own. But the real Christian repeats the divine words, "Ye were bought with a price; therefore, glorify God in your body and in your spirit, which are God's."

Now it is the duty and privilege of each one of us to make known to the world, to **all** the world, this gift of God, this good-will to men, and to live a life of good-will of giving and of service, to do in Christ's name as His representative what He did and is doing on earth. Not a selfish salvation, a saving merely of our own self-centered souls; but a salvation for one great purpose only—power to win others to Christ, and to train them up in Christ, and to send them out for Christ. We need this kind of a life, not merely that we may be saved at last, but that we may make our lives count for the eternal enrichment of all lives that we touch.

Feeble, are we? Yes, without God we are nothing, but what by faith every man may be, God requires him to be. And what a reckoning will it be for many of us when Christ summons us to answer before him, under His law, not for what we are, but for what we might have been.

The Love of Christ to His People
Maud E. Hoyle

(This is the first regular sermon delivered at the Columbus Avenue United Brethren Church, Springfield, Ohio, when it opened its doors on August 27, 1912. It was read again at the last church service held there on December 27, 2009.)

I do not come to you as one who is perfect or as one who knows a great deal. But one thing I do know is that God has forgiven my sins and that I now love Him with my whole heart, and I am trying to daily live as He would have me live.

Most of you who are present have known me since I was a little girl, and therefore I hesitate somewhat in coming before you. But I want you to forget the speaker as far as possible and let us together turn our attention to God and His message to us.

The subject of the message is LOVE. The theme is THE LOVE OF CHRIST TO HIS PEOPLE. The text is found in John 15:9: "As the Father hath loved Me, so have I loved you. Continue ye in My love."

The Savior is discoursing in this chapter on the union subsisting between Himself and His believing people. He likens Himself to the vine, His people to the branches, and shows how entirely they depend upon Him for fruitfulness and safety: "I am the vine, ye are the branches; He that abideth in me, and I in him, the same beareth much fruit; for apart from me ye can do nothing; if a man abide not in me, he is cast forth as a branch and is withered, and men gather them, and cast them into the fire, and they are burned."

He then shows how the Father would be glorified in their bearing much fruit and states they might ask in prayer as largely and abundantly as they pleased. "If ye abide in me, and my words abide in you, ask whatsoever ye will, and it shall be done unto you. Herein is my Father glorified, that ye bear much fruit, and so shall ye be my disciples." Then it is that He declares unto them the affectionate sentiment of the text. "As the Father hath loved me, I also have loved you; abide ye in my love." The subject contains:

I. A Gracious Declaration

II. An Interesting Similitude

III. An Affectionate Exhortation

I. "I have loved you" is the gracious declaration! Christ's love is the very essence of the gospel; as without this no tidings of great joy would ever have been communicated to perishing man. The love of Christ is evident from the professions of His love. The name He assumed was a profession of His love. Have you ever noticed how often the expression "His name" or "In His name" is used in the Bible? It occurs in different connections over 100 times. He was called Jesus because He came to save His people from their sins. The professions of love to man He revealed by the prophets; they all testified of Christ, and His love to the sons of men.

When Christ appeared in our nature, He manifested the most ardent attachment to our race. In Jesus, men saw a living picture of God. He was God in such form that human eyes could look upon Him and human ears could hear Him speak and human hearts love Him. But God was the same God before they had this picture. And so is He still; and God is our salvation. Jesus was the perfect revelation of God. I wish you would try to imagine how the people who knew Jesus best at the time He was here in body must have learned to love Him. He not only told them wonderful secrets respecting life, which caused them to think life worth living, but He lived this life before them. But it was not for His life alone that they loved Him, but for Himself. He was ever thinking of them. He appeared bound up in love to them. He was ready to add to their comfort at any cost to Himself. Though they called him "Master," He was among them as one who served.

Christ exhorted them, wooed them, wept over them, went about healing their sicknesses, removing their misery, and forgiving their sins. How could they help loving Him with a love stronger than death? At one time when He was about to start on a dangerous journey, they said, "Let us go also and die with Him." At length He began to talk to them of being crucified and parting from them. Upon hearing this, they were in deep sorrow, until He unfolded to them His plan of returning in spirit and so of being ever with them. This came about. He returned in spirit. Most wonderful happiness followed, and it was now that they began to tell others of Him. It was on one of the first of these occasions that Peter said, "Neither is there salvation in any other, for there is none other name under heaven, given among men whereby we must be saved." He spoke of something which the disciples all knew, for in Jesus, they felt that they had found everything the heart could desire.

All of His Apostles testify of His professed love to mankind. "Herein is love," they say, "not that we loved God, but that He loved us and sent His Son to be the propitiation for our sins." Unto Him that loved us and washed us from our sins in His own blood." Then His discourses, His miracles, his prayers all proved the truth and sincerity of His love toward us.

The achievements of His love: His love was affective, it produced the most glorious consequences to mankind. I tell you there is nothing that can compensate the Church, or the individual Christian, for the lack of the Holy Spirit. We shall stand powerless and abashed in the presence of our difficulties and our foes, until we learn what He can be as a mighty tide of love and power in our hearts. The Pentecostal fullness, the endowment of power, the baptism of fire are all within our reach. Let us be inspired with a holy ambition to get all that our God is willing and eager to bestow.

God is love: We cannot dwell with Him without sharing this attribute. We have all watched the growth of loveliness in lives unlovely by nature. Association with Christ promotes likeness to Christ.

His love magnified the law and removed the curse—His love made Him our surety, and He bore the pain, endured the cross, despised the shame, and made His soul an offering for sin. Yes, He loved us and gave Himself for us. His loved induced Him to become our deliverer, to encounter the foes of our race, and to overcome for our salvation, sin, death, and the grave. Yes, He spoiled our adversary. He led the captive from captivity, overcame principalities and powers, and made a show of them openly.

The provisions of His love: His love has not only achieved much but provided for us the unsearchable riches of grace here, and of glory in the world to come. The blessings are too numerous to be named, so I will mention only a few as specimen.

Pardon—God forgives—forgives not just as a sudden impulse of the mind, a mere whim, but with wise, definite Divine prearrangement; forgives universally on the ground of an atonement, and on the condition of repentance and faith.

Peace—Matthew Henry says that when Christ was about to leave the world, He made His will. His soul He committed to His Father; His body He bequeathed to Joseph to be decently interred; His clothes fell to the soldiers; His mother He left to the care of John; but what should He leave to His poor disciples that had left all for Him. Silver and gold, He had none; but He left them that which was infinitely better, His peace. "My peace I give to you." How different the peace of God from that of the world! It calms the passions, preserves the purity of the conscience, is inseparable from righteousness, unites us to God and strengthens us against temptations. The peace of the soul consists in an absolute resignation to the will of God.

Then there is *righteousness, joy, immortality.* Immortality! We bow before the very term. Love does not argue. Love trusts, and love's argument for the hope of immortality is a deathless faith. Until the child thought becomes influenced by the thought of older persons, it does not "think death." The little maid, in Wordsworth's, "We Are Seven," is a type of all children.

In *The Outlook* was an article entitled "What Children Like to Read." An incident was related of a girl who was fond of memorizing verses. She would often offer to say poetry to her neighbor. One afternoon, she stood at the window for a time, looking silently out at the leaves whirling and rustling in the trees dark against the sunset sky. She began to repeat "The Death of the Flowers" by William Cullen Bryant. With the last stanza, her voice changed slightly. "I love this part," she interrupted herself to say:

> And then I think of one, who in her youthful beauty died,
> The fair, meek blossom that grew up and faded by my side:
> In the cold, moist earth we laid her, when the forest cast its leaf,
> And we wept that one so lovely should have a life so brief:
> Yet not unmeet, it was one, like that young friend of ours,
> So gentle and so beautiful, should perish with the flowers.

"Why do you like that part? It is so sad," she was asked. The little girl looked in amazement. "Do you think it sad? I think it is comforting. It makes me feel that she—the little girl in the poem, you know, wasn't hurt by dying any more than the flowers are. You know, they'll all come alive in the spring."

This is the comfort of resurrection, *hope*. A great host of friends awaits us—parents, brothers, sisters, children—secure in the blessed immortality, awaiting the time of rejoicing, when we shall renew society with our loved ones on immortal shores. "Eye hath not seen, nor ear heard, neither have entered into the heart of man, the things which God hath prepared for them that love Him."

II. What has been advanced respecting Christ's love, may scripturally apply to all mankind. Remember the whosoevers of John. But He displays peculiar and special love to those who have believed on His name. These He loves with complacency and delight and it is to these that our attention is expressly called in the second part of the subject. Notice them in the text: An Interesting Similitude. "As the Father hath loved me, so have I loved you." This agreement between God's love to His Son, and the love of Christ to His people may include:

1. The antiquity of His love. Christ said to the Father, "Thou lovedst me before the foundation of the world" (John 27:14). So, Christ loved the Church and His delights were with His people from everlasting. "Yea, I have loved thee with an everlasting love," saith Jehovah.

2. This may refer to the ground of His love. The ground of the Father's love to Christ was the express image He bore of Himself. This likeness consists in being of one mind with Jesus, obeying His holy commandments and following in His steps. He loves us because we are His. We are His by creation. His image and superscription have been stamped upon every lineament of our face, though almost obliterated, as the image of the sovereign from a well-worn coin. "It is He who has made us, and we are His."

Jesus became incarnate that He might redeem us to Himself, a peculiar people, zealous of good works, and that they might be partakers of the divine nature. So, we are His, not only by creation, but by the purchase; for never was slave more certainly acquired by silver and

THE LOVE OF CHRIST TO HIS PEOPLE | 171

gold than we have been bought by His precious blood. "Ye are not your own, ye are bought with a price, wherefore glorify God in your body and spirit, which are His."

We are His by deed of gift, for the Father has given to Him all who shall come to Him and it is impossible to believe that this donation could be anything less that our whole being. When God gave us, He gave all of us. We are His by conquest; it is impossible to escape the fact that in the thought of God and according to the rights of the case, we are the absolute property of Jesus Christ, our Lord, and that He thinks much of that fact is evident in the frequent references of His high priest by prayer (John 17) though we, I am afraid, are often too forgetful of his claims.

3. It may include as a similitude the greatness of God's love. The Father loved the Son with an inexpressible love. In like manner, Christ hath loved His people; and His love in its length and breadth, and depth, and height passeth knowledge. He loved them so as to lay down His life and shed His precious blood for them.

4. It may apply to the constancy of His love. The Father loved the son always. His love never wavered nor abated for a single moment. So, Christ having loved His own, which are in the world, He loved them to the end. Yes, He loves you in all seasons and circumstances, in health, in sickness, death and eternity.

5. And how did the Father show His love to His Son? What were the evidences of His love? He always heard Him. You remember the grave of Lazarus after they had removed the stone. Jesus lifted His eyes and said, "Father, I thank thee that thou hast heard me and I know that thou hearest me always." He was ever with Him. In John 16:32, we read that just before His arrest, He said to His disciples, "Behold the hour cometh, yea, is now come that ye shall be scattered, every man to His own, and shall leave me alone, and yet I am not alone,

because the Father is with Me." He gave all things into His hands, the Father loveth the Son and hath given all things into His hand (John 3:35), so Jesus ever hears His people. He is with them always. He has made them heirs of all things. All are yours, and ye are Christ's and Christ is God's. We are heirs of God and joint heirs with Christ.

6. And then it may include in the sixth place, the glorious rewards of His love. The Father has given Him a name above every name, raised him to great power and dominion; and has glorified Him with the glory which He had with Him before the world was. Yet similar glory does Christ give to His people. In the Lord's prayer as recorded in John 17, He says, "And the glory which thou gavest me, I have given them." Then in Revelation, "To him that overcometh will I grant to sit with me in my throne, even as I also overcame and am set down with my Father in His throne."

III. And now in the last place, let us notice with what an affectionate exhortation He closes. In the first place, He gives the declaration, "I have loved you." In the second place, He shows them that His love for them is similar to the Father's love to Himself, "As my Father hath loved me, so have I loved you." Then He closes with this exhortation: "Continue ye in my love."

Continue to prize and value His love. What else is so worthy of our highest joys and delight? Jesus is the same comforting, helping, instructing, loving Elder Brother as when John leaned on His bosom, as when He lifted Peter up from the waves, as when He dried Mary's tears with His "Thy sins are forgiven thee." Jesus is the same almighty Savior, Guide, Intercessor as when He ascended to glory with the broken fetters of sin and death in His pierced hands. To multitudes of sufferers on beds of pain and languishing, Jesus has been still the great Physician today; in many a weeping circle around precious dust, He has been the Divine Comforter in your home, in mine, and tears almost ceased to flow as this Jesus has touched the casket. Dying lips have whispered His name in your home, and in mine, and the valley of the shadow has been lit up as with the glory from the heavenly shores.

So therefore, continue to cultivate it. It is a holy, tender affection, and must be nurtured with the greatest care. You may be quite sure that if little light comes from a Christian character, little light comes into it. We must have the glory sink into us, then cultivate it before it can be reflected from us. Did you ever think of the reason why the Psalms of David have come, like beacon lights, down across the ages, why they make the keynote of grateful piety in every Christian's soul, wherever He lives? It is because they are so full of gratitude. "Oh, that men would praise the Lord for His goodness and for His wonderful works to the children of men." Let us seek, as a plain duty, to cultivate a buoyant, joyous sense of the crowded kindnesses of God in our daily lives, and thus, show to the world that we are abiding in His love.

Let us continue to abound more and more in it. May we make advances, grow in grace and in the knowledge of our Lord Jesus Christ. May our fellowship to Him become closer day by day.

Let us continue to give evidence of it, by walking as He walked. Neighbors and friends, don't you know that the strongest argument for the truth of Christianity is the true Christian ones who are filled with the spirit of Christ? The best proof of Christ's resurrection is a living Church, which itself is walking in a new life, and drawing life from Him who hath overcome death. He that saith, be abideth in Him ought himself also to walk even as He walked. The Christian is the world's Bible. Men of the world do not read God's word to find out what is religion. They look to the life and conduct of those who profess to believe it. A good life is the most powerful preaching. Many a man has been led to Christ by the consistent life of one of His followers. So, let us be careful how we walk in our daily life, in the home, in the school, in the shop, in the market, or wherever we may be. We can do this alright only as we abide in His love, but keeping His commandments, loving one another, and promoting His cause.

Now we continue to profess and recommend it. Be Christ's witnesses. You cannot find, I believe, a case in the Bible where a man is converted without God's calling in some human agency, using some human instrument. It is through the mass of living human hearts, of human acts, and words of love and truth that the Christ of the first century has become Christ of the twentieth. What if every Christian would say, "Lord I want a revival and let it begin in me. Give me the earnestness, faith, and tenderness that I am looking for in others. Make me such a devoted worker as I think others ought to be. Let the revival begin in me and begin now."

Do not be ashamed to confess that you have accepted Him. What we want above all things are men and women with a high aim, zealous to have Christ's name glorified and souls saved. Men and women who know Christ inwardly, and stand for Him outwardly.

Conclusion:

1. Friends, do not despise Christ's love to you. Pray God that He will root out of our hearts everything of our own planting, and set out there, with His own hands the tree of life, bearing all manner of fruits.

2. Those who are sad, lift up your heads and be happy in the provisions this love has made.

3. Disciples of Christ, rejoice in this love with joy unspeakable and full of glory. Rejoice in Christ Jesus, for in Him you are complete. His righteousness is over you;

His strong arm is around you, and He who puts his soul in Christ's keeping shall never perish nor come into condemnation. This is a safe place to rest in.

Who shall separate us from the love of Christ?

The Lord is Looking
Maud E. Hoyle

(While no date is given for this sermon, the mention of "the Home" indicates that Maud delivered it sometime between 1945 -1958 while she lived at the Otterbein Home. This is the last known sermon of Maud's.)

Text: "And Jesus entered into Jerusalem, and into the temple: and when he had looked round about upon all things, and now the eventide was come, he went out unto Bethany with the twelve." (Mark 11:11)

Jesus entered into Jerusalem and into the temple and looked round about upon all things. The secular and religious life of the place were being watched and weighed that day. Even without pictorial help, you can imagine the divine Observer, that face which no hand can paint—silent, eager, and sad—moving through the city streets and the temple courts, looking round about upon all things. The day that Jesus entered the town and the temple was a solemn day. That day, the work and worship of Jerusalem was examined by him whom we call Master and Lord.

The first thought suggests our unconsciousness of the Divine presence. We are not sufficiently aware that the Lord stands watching our lives. True, there are pure-minded Christians who live with such devotion and truth and uprightness that their whole life seems spent in the Light of God's countenance, but the greater part of many lives is passed as if men thought the omniscient Sentinel were off his guard. We are unaware of the presence of the Lord.

In ancient ages, God had come among the people of Israel and now Jesus came. Formerly God had looked upon them from a pillar of fire; now he watched them through two human eyes. The people never thought how perfectly his gaze was focused on the place.

Tomorrow, it will be similar in our case. We shall know that God is looking, but we have grown accustomed to that fact; we grow used to everything. Familiarity wears away impressions. Do you remember when you first came to the Home? Everything was so different. But be here sufficiently long and these become familiar sights, and their weird spell departs. Even so, with God's life-truths, we grow accustomed to these deep and sacred things. Do you suppose we should think much of the pillar of fire, if we gazed on its crimson glow every night? Or of the manna, if we trod on its pearly bead every morning? If one rose from the dead, we should repent—but not if he came often—not if he stayed long.

Here, boys and girls, men and women, here, this morning is the peril of our souls. Truth fell among the thorns, and the thorns sprang up and choked it. The truth of God's Word becomes blunt unless we take heed. Our daily prayers, communions, readings, hymns, and sermons are all designed to give buried truth resurrection. Whoever would not be blind to God must often "go wash in the pool of Siloam."

Two disciples walked a road with Jesus at their side "but their eyes were holden that they should not know him." Many of us travel life's highway without realizing an unseen Lord challenging our earth-filled vision. Once to a woman Jesus said, "If thou knewest *who* it is that saith to thee, 'Give me to drink,' thou wouldst ask of him." Ah! *If thou knewest who it is.* If the people of Jerusalem, at whom Jesus looked that day, could have realized *who* looked through the quiet eyes of that Galilean, they would have cried, "Thou God seest me!" But, "he was in the world and world knew him not." Oh, Lord that we might receive our sight!

The second thought is the thoroughness of our Lord's observation. "He looked round about upon all things." It was Passover time. Jerusalem was choked with strangers. Boys came with their eager first look at the marble and gold. Old men came laden with hallowed remembrances and wondering if they would ever again see "the city of the great King." Jewish nature is human nature. Some of these pilgrims were made better for the journey, while others continued to find Jerusalem anything but a city of God while they were there. Naturally enough, the Jewish residents would not miss their chance while strangers were there. The fishermen were busy with their nets. The city and temple; the secular and religious life. We split life into two halves. Certain things such as singing hymns, praying, and listening to sermons are religious; while day work in the world, money-making, school work, are secular. Our New Testament is flat against this heathen separating! "Whatsoever we do in word or deed, we do all in the name of the Lord Jesus" and "the Earth is the Lord's and the fulness thereof." We spend one day in God's house (or perhaps half a day) and six days in God's world. Sunday is not the scapegoat of our past six days, but the inspiration of our six days to come. The temple of God is nothing except she became the foster mother to the city of God. Town and temple Jesus enters into. He looked about at all things, knowing the hidden motives. What a terrible thing is the ill opinion of a community for one to stand exposed and characterless, but to stand thus before an omnipresent God, is not that dreadful?

The third thought has to do with the sympathy with which our lives are watched. Jesus looked. Do not think we live under the observation of a spy. He who looked over Jerusalem *wept* over it. He who looked at all things, overlooked no good thing. Jesus sat the next day "over against the treasury looking." He saw a poor widow give those two mites and he spoke of that in such a way that it will be heard through all generations. Some day we will find out Jesus has missed no good thing. When seated on the throne of His glory, he will say to those on his right hand, "Come, ye blessed of my Father... for I was hungry, and ye gave me meat: I was thirsty, and ye gave me drink: I was a stranger, and ye took me in; naked, and ye clothed me; I was sick, and ye visited me; I was in prison, and ye came unto me." We will answer when? When? When? "In as much as ye did it unto the least of these, ye did it unto me."

I do not speak of willful errors and sins against the known will of God. These are not faults but crimes against the kingdom of heaven. "He knows our frame and remembers that we are dust." If any eye can compensate human frailty, it must be the eye of Him who died for us. It is better to fall into the hand of God than of men. "Thou God seest me."

"Jesus looked round about upon all things." How *still* he is though? Sometimes he says nothing, does nothing, but merely looks. This silence of the Lord is a great mystery to our thoughts and a great trial to our faiths. Why is he so still? Why does he not interfere? Why not unmask the pretender in the church? Why not put things right in the city? Why is He so still? This mystery is a common experience. You see an illustration of this in the story of Bethany. "When Jesus had heard, therefore, that Lazarus was sick, he abode two days still in the same place where he was." And the poor sisters said, "Lord, if thou hadst been here, our brother had not died." The Jews in that little country graveyard talked of this mystery. *But He let him die* and He knew why. The Lord knows and he only, why his swift helpfulness sometimes pauses at a distance from distress as if his hour had not yet come. He will come, but *we* think he ought to come more quickly. But he says, rebuking our impatience, "What I do thou knowest not now, but though shalt know hereafter... Stand still and see the salvation of God."

Jesus entered into the city and into the temple and looked round about upon all things. Write that truth in your heart and let it talk with you by the way. The truth may be either life's sweetest comfort or its sternest terror. You may put yourself in what relationship to Him you choose, either that of a child whom He protects or a prisoner whom he follows with a slowly accumulating vengeance. The Lord watches the good as the Saviour. He compasses the wicked with a fiery ring. Answer His look with the cry, "Lord what wilt thou have me do?"

History of the Columbus Avenue United Brethren Church – 1918
(with a 1935 addendum)

Maud E. Hoyle

About the year 1900, it pleased the Lord God to awaken persons in this community who should raise up a Bible School. These persons obeyed the call of their Lord and Master. Their labors were blessed, and they established a Bible School in Benson's School House. This school continued until 1908, when it was discontinued for lack of workers. The Lord called them again so strongly that they decided to devote their strength to His service.

Cottage prayer meetings were being held every Tuesday evening. Religious enthusiasm increased, and at the July 15, 1911 Quarterly Conference of the Lagonda United Brethren Church, Maud E. Hoyle (she being a local minister of that church) asked for advice concerning a Bible School in this community. Rev. C. W. Kurtz, the presiding elder of the conference, and Dr. Klinefelter, pastor of the church, selected a committee of three men—James Barclay, John Ober, and John Laybourn—to solicit and give their opinion as to the advisability of building in this community and to report at the next Quarterly Conference.

The report being favorable, a committee of men looked about for a good location. The lot was purchased from Harry Kohl, Sr, for $1.50 per running foot front, with 127 ft. purchased and paid for. At the Quarterly Conference held January 27, 1912, the following trustees were selected: Frank Getz for 5 years, Frank Wallace, 4 years, Wilson Hinman, 3 years, Harry Kohl, Sr, 2 yrs, and Fred Weaver, 1 year. These trustees were legally incorporated at Columbus, Ohio. Mrs. James Barclay, Mrs. Frank Getz, and Maud Hoyle were appointed as a finance committee.

March 4, 1912, the ground was broken after a short but impressive ceremony. Rev. B. F. Farris, pastor of Lagonda Church was in charge.

> Song – Higher Ground
> Prayer and address based on Ps. 127:1 – Rev. Farris
> The first shovel full of dirt was carried from foundation space by Maud Hoyle.
> Song – I Want to Be a Worker – with joined hands.
> Prayer – Maud Hoyle

Those present were Rev. Farris, Fred Weaver, Mr. & Mrs. Harry Kohl, Sr., Mrs. Greenler, Mr. & Mrs. Grant Kimble, Simon Fox, Mr. & Mrs. J. B. Wallace, Mrs. James Barclay, Mrs. James Truman, Mrs. S. U. Hoyle, Maud Hoyle, Frank Wallace, Mr. & Mrs. Bert Wallace, Elwood Wallace, and Bernice Wallace.

Another red-letter day was March 20, 1912. Unusual interest marked the services held at 1:30 p.m. for the corner-stone laying. Some 50 persons joined in the celebration. The church never was more in earnest or deeply spiritual. Rev. Farris of Lagonda United Brethren Church had charge of the service, assisted by Rev. Maud Hoyle.

> Reading of Discipline – Rev. Farris
> Song – I Love Thy Church Oh, God
> Scripture Lesson – 1 Cor. 3:9 – Maud Hoyle
> Sentence prayers
> Address – Rev. Farris
> Prayer – Rev. Farris
> History of the Church – Maud Hoyle
> Filling of the box (jar)
> Rev. Farris then proceeded with the ceremony
> Benediction – Maud Hoyle

Contents of Jar:
Bible – Edna Farris
Discipline – Maud Hoyle
Telescope – Mrs. S. U. Hoyle
Watchword –
Evangel – Mrs. Grant Kimble
History of Church – Maud Hoyle
Message to Future Pastors – Rev. Farris
Picture of Evelyn Hinman, 3 yrs. old
Old coins –
    2 - 1¢ – Harry Kohl, Sr.
    2¢ – Harry Kohl, Sr.
    1¢ – James Barclay
    Pennies – Mrs. Turner, Mrs. Weaver, Mrs. Martin, Mrs. S. U. Hoyle, Mrs. Taylor, Mr. Taylor, Charles Martin, Bert Wallace
    10¢ – Mrs. J. B. Wallace
Names of families – Frank and Bert Wallace
Jar that held these was given as a tribute to Mrs. A. Allen – deceased.

Those present were Rev. B. F. Farris, Mrs. Lillie Turner, Mrs. Leonard Truman, Mrs. Guy Truman, Frederick Getz, Mr. & Mrs. Harry Kohl, Sr., Mr. & Mrs. Grant Kimble, Mr. & Mrs. James Truman, Mr. & Mrs. Bert Wallace, Mr. & Mrs. Wilson Hinman, Frank Getz, Mrs. Geo. Arnett, Jr., Saben Coffee, Mrs. W. J. Hoyle and Robert, Lillie May, Robert and Charles Wallace, Elwood, Francis, Irene, and Bernice Wallace, Mrs. Geo Arnett, Sr., Mrs. Frank Martin, Mrs. Frank Lindemann and 2 children, Mrs. Bert Hough and mother, Mr. & Mrs. S. U. Hoyle and Maud, Harry Kohl, Jr., Samuel Barclay, Irvin Kimble.

From the first, the work moved along splendidly. Though the work has been hard, the men and women toiled unceasingly, persistently, and heroically. The Church was built largely by donated labor of the members and friends of the church. Mr. James Truman donated his time to oversee the carpenter work. Special mention should be given Mrs. Laura Arnett and Mrs. Lillie Turner. These two women of God seemed tireless in their efforts, going forward where none other thought of advancement, and God rewarded their efforts.

The following families have given of their time, strength, and means: James Barclay, Frank Getz, Fred Weaver, Bert Hough, Mrs. Lillie Turner, J. B. Wallace, S. U. Hoyle, Frank Wallace, Wilson Hinman, Miss Ellen Eberly, Leonard Truman, Harry Kohl, Mr. Koener, Mrs. Rice, Walter Hoyle, Wilbur Hoyle, Ashby Allender, D. D. Trombley, John Marcum, G. W. Arnett, Sr., G. W. Arnett, Jr., Percy Runyan, J. S. Swaidner, Bert Wallace, Edward Frock, Mrs. W. Crouse, J. S. Gochenour, Frank Lindemann, Charles Alsheimer, Saben Coffee, Frank Lee, Samuel Barclay, James Truman, Roy Jones, William Mumper, Homer Barclay, Samuel Tobias, D. H. Olds, Miss Anna Kelly, Simon Fox, Claude Allen, Albert Getz, William Clark, Geo. McKaig, Milton Laython, Mrs. Leola Scott, B. F. Whittington, Grant Kimble, Frank Martin, Irvin Kimble.

The house was completed with basement and furnace and seating capacity of 250. The building cost $2,500.

Kerosene lamps were first in use, followed in time by a gasoline lighting system. When electricity was available, the lighting system was changed again.

The first service held in the church was a prayer meeting, August 27, 1912, led by Maud Hoyle. September 8, 1912, the Sunday School was organized with 134 members, Church class with 51 members, Christian Endeavor with 34 members, and Ladies Aid with 37 members. Rev. B. F. Farris, pastor of the Lagonda United Brethren Church, was in charge of this service. His subject was "The Church of Christ." (Matthew 16:18).

The first quarterly conference was held November 1, 1912, and the church was dedicated November 3, 1912. Both services were conducted by Dr. C. W. Kurtz, Conference Superintendent.

At a special meeting, January 3, 1915, the property and building being free of debt; the note was burned by the trustees. After the flames died down, it was discovered one word remained — that word was "paid."

Dr. Kurtz was a great help to the new organization, giving sound advice and encouragement. He preached his last sermon at this church. The fourth Quarterly Conference was held August 4, 1918. Dr. Kurtz presided. After the service, he went to the home of Wilbur Hoyle for the night. The following morning, he was stricken while working with his machine, preparatory to going to his next appointment. He died in the Springfield City Hospital after a few days, but never regained consciousness.

The parsonage was built in 1918 at a cost of $2,500. Much of the labor and some material were donated. It was dedicated October 13, 1918, by Supt. A. R. Clippinger.

There has been enough success to encourage and enough failure to keep us humble. May these beginnings promote better acquaintance and aid in quickening zeal for future enlargement and so lead to the praise of Him, Whom we love and serve.

The Charter Members were: Mrs. Laura Arnett, Mrs. Alexander, Mr. and Mrs. James Barclay, Mr. and Mrs. Charles Dersch, Mr. and Mrs. Albert Goetz, Mr. and Mrs. Frank Goetz, Mr. and Mrs. Wilson Hinman, Mr. and Mrs. Frank Martin, Mr. and Mrs. John Marcum, Mr. and Mrs. Percy Runyan, Mr. and Mrs. James Truman, Mr. and Mrs. Leonard Truman, Mr. and Mrs. Guy Truman, Mr. and Mrs. J. B. Wallace, Mr. and Mrs. Frank Wallace, Mr. and Mrs. Bert Wallace, Mr. and Mrs. Fred Weaver, Mr. and Mrs. Charles Weaver, Mrs. Lillie Turnery, Forest Barclay, Lloyd Barclay, Emma Barclay, Lillie Barclay, Charley Barclay, Alice Burkhardt, Mildred Eleyet, Mrs. S. U. Hoyle, Maud Hoyle, McKay Runyan, Philip Runyan,

Marjory Runyan, Philip Runyan, Mrs. Leola Scott, Irene Trombley, Joice Trombley.

Addition to History

In the previous account of this organization, written by Miss Maud Hoyle, she has in her reserve and modesty practically submerged the fact that she is the promoter of the Columbus Avenue United Brethren Chapel. Since this is so, the undersigned feels that this notation should be added —

Mr. Wilson Hinman, a charter member had written this:

"History of Columbus Avenue United Brethren Chapel and tribute to its Founder, Miss Maud Hoyle, for had it not have been for the untiring efforts of the latter, there probably would be no history to write.

"As it is well known that from the beginning of time, God raised up men and women to carry out His program, and assuredly as He laid His hand on Philip William Otterbein and Martin Boehm, so did He call Miss Maud Hoyle to further His Kingdom by founding Columbus Avenue United Brethren Chapel."

The church asked Miss Hoyle to make up this record, instructing Wilson Hinman to prepare an introductory, but Maud submerged this, because it referred to herself.

Since her last return from Africa, in 1930, she has been almost the constant caretaker of her aged mother, Mrs. Ida Hoyle. In spite of this, she has in these years since aided the foundation with the recording of the membership here. As an assist to her, the undersigned has in this month of August gathered further statistics.

Future pastors should enter new members in record as they are received and gather further statistics.

Written this second day of August 1935.

Rev. A. J. Furstenberger

Pastor 1930-1935

Appendices

Appendix A:
Abbreviated HOYLE Family Genealogy Chart
(Names appearing in this book are in bold face)

Stephen and Ida (Dowden) Hoyle
- **Walter** (and **Lida** Garrety)
  - **Chester**
  - **Arthur** (and Alice Ogle)
    - **Susan**
    - Sharon
  - Robert (and Violet Armacost)
    - Robert, Jr.
  - Walter (and Martha Fox)
    - Stephanie
    - Joseph
    - Walter Gerald
    - Sandra
    - David
  - **Dorothy** (and Verlon Dale Cash)
    - **Sheila**
    - Sharilyn
    - **Michele**
- **Wilbur** (and **Henrietta** Fissel)
  - **Paul** (and Elizabeth Steiner)
    - **John**
    - Mary Ann
  - **Helen**
  - Elizabeth (and Warren Sutton)
    - Stephen
    - Shirley
- **Maud**
- **Charlotte**

Appendix B:
Boxwell-Patterson Examination, April 19, 1902

The following is taken from Henry Graham Williams' compilation, *Boxwell-Patterson Examinations: Being a Complete List of All Questions Issued by the State Commissioner of Schools Since the Patterson Law Went Into Effect. Comp. for the Use of Teachers Who Are Preparing Pupils for the Patterson Examinations Or for Admission to High School, And for Pupils for Home Study.* Athens, O.: The Ohio Teacher, 1912.

EIGHTH GRADE EXAMINATIONS
BOXWELL-PATTERSON EXAMINATIONS

Pupils' Examination— April 19, 1902.
(Under Act of March 28, 1902.)

ORTHOGRAPHY.

1. Make and name the ordinary punctuation marks.
2. Mark diacritically the following words: visual, calico, aisle, air, coordinate.
3. Give the force and meaning of the following affixes: con, anti, ly, ing and ad.
4. Spell the following words to be pronounced by the examiner: (1)business (2)until (3)bureau (4)niece (5)supersede (6)separate (7)isolate (8)cemetery (9)souvenir (10)synopsis (11)privilege (12)deceive (13)diphtheria (14)neuralgia (15)hygiene (16)tomato (17)sycamore (18)Constantinople (19)Marseilles (20)Cincinnati.
5. Select eight of the above words and give their definition.

READING.

Oral reading from standard authors to be conducted by the examiners.

WRITING.

1. The general character of the manuscripts will be used in part in determining the grade in this branch.
2. Copy the following quotation in your best handwriting:
    Sunset and evening star
        And one clear call for me;
    And may there be no moaning of the bar
        When I put out to sea.
    But such a tide as moving seems asleep.
        Too full for sound and foam.
    When that which drew from out the boundless deep.
        Turns again home.
                    -- Tennyson.

ARITHMETIC.

1. Define factor, ratio, commission, least common multiple, interest.
2. How do you find the cost price when the selling price and rate of gain are given? How do you find the present worth of a debt?
3. I sold an article for $17.50 and lost 12 ½ per cent.; what per cent, would I have gained or lost had I sold it for $15.00?

4. $\dfrac{\frac{1/2 \text{ of } 5/6}{2/3}}{\frac{1}{2}} \div \dfrac{\frac{¾ \times 5/6}{2}}{3/4 \div 1\,1/2} = ?$

5. I gave my agent $162.50 with which to buy corn at 62 1/4 cents a bushel, after deducting his commission of 4 per cent. How many bushels did he buy?
6. Express in figures: one hundred and seven thousand two hundred and six and eighteen ten-thousandths; one hundred and seven thousand two hundred and six ten-

millionths. Express in words: 298.015; 500.01025; 1256.081.
7. How many bushels of wheat can be put in a bin 8 feet square and 9 feet high?
8. What are the proceeds of a note of $142.00 dated August 15, 1901, and payable November 4, 1901, discounted at 10 per cent.?
9. Find the area in acres of a piece of land .5 mile long and .3 mile broad.
10. I owned 5/8 of a farm and sold 2/5 of my share to A, who then had 40 acres less than I had left. How many acres in the farm?

GRAMMAR AND COMPOSITION.

1. Write a sentence that will contain a noun in the objective case, a noun in apposition, a. pronoun in the possessive case, and a descriptive adjective.
2. Write a synopsis of the verb sing in the third person, singular number, active and passive voice, indicative mood.
3. What is a direct object? An indirect object? A predicate object?
Write sentences to illustrate each.
4. What are relative pronouns? Name them. To what does each refer for antecedent?
5. What are subordinate clauses? Causal clauses? Clauses of purpose? Write an example of each.
6. What are the parts of a letter? Illustrate by writing a letter to Mr. John Newton, 89 State St., Boston, Mass., telling him something of your school work this year.
7. Answer the following invitation: Mrs. James Logan requests the pleasure of Miss Adams's company at dinner on Wednesday, April thirteenth, at six o'clock. 239 Main Street.
8. Tell the case of the nouns and pronouns in the following sentences: I asked John to bring me a drink

of water. Washington, with his defeated army, was in the city of New York, just after the battle of Long Island.
9. Analyze or diagram the following: Captain Nathan Hale, a brilliant and handsome young man, came forward and said, "I will undertake it." His last words were, "I regret that I have but one life to lose for my country."
10. What are conditional clauses? Indirect questions? Write an example of each.

GEOGRAPHY.

(Select any eight questions.)
1. What is longitude? Through what grand divisions does the parallel of 30° north latitude pass? 30° south latitude? Through what grand division does the meridian of 30° east longitude pass? 30° west longitude?
2. Name five railroads in Ohio which run into Chicago. Name three great lines of railroad running from Chicago to the great West.
3. In which states are the largest forests row found? Where is the most coffee raised? The most tea? The most rice?
4. Locate: St. Louis, Minneapolis, Manila, Milan, Yellowstone Park, Name one fact in connection with each.
5. Draw an outline map of Ohio and locate in it three of the largest rivers and five of the largest cities.
6. Into which ocean do the large rivers of the world flow? Why? Name the mountain ranges running from Spain eastward through southern Europe and Asia.
7. Where would you go to see the following: Bunker Hill Monument? Garfield's Monument? Mammoth Cave? Tower of Pisa? Garden of the Gods? The Erie Canal? Lookout Mountain? Harvard College? Statue of Liberty? Falls of Minnehaha?

8. What is meant by "standard time"? What is climate? Soil? Rock? River system?
9. What crops are being harvested at this season of the year in Australia? How would you go from Columbus to Manila?
10. How do you account for the size of the following cities: Paris? New York? New Orleans? Minneapolis? Philadelphia?

UNITED STATES HISTORY, INCLUDING CIVIL GOVERNMENT.

1. What was there in the life and deeds of the following that you think commendable? William Penn? John Smith? Roger Williams? U. S. Grant?
2. Why did the southern states claim the right to secede from the Union? Which states seceded? Name five important battles of the Civil War.
3. With what event in history is the name of each associated: Balboa? De Soto? Cyrus Field? Alexander Hamilton? Daniel Webster?
4. When was the Northwest territory set apart? Name the states made from it, giving their capitals.
5. Name the six provisions of Clay's Compromise of 1850.
6. What difficulties were experienced under "The Articles of Confederation"?
7. Name the chief powers of Congress.
8. What is meant by the Electoral College? What are its duties and how performed?

PHYSIOLOGY.

1. How are bones nourished? How is a broken bone repaired?
2. What office does the skin perform? The tendons?
3. Describe the alimentary canal.
4. Trace the blood from the right hand to the left hand.

5. Name three narcotics. What organ is first affected by narcotics?
6. What would you do for a fainting person? How would you stop bleeding from an artery? From a vein?
7. What is the object of respiration and what are the organs of respiration? What are some of the evils of mouth-breathing?
8. What can you state as to the habits of people living in different climates, in respect to diet?
9. What is the value of sugar as a food? Why is a mixed diet necessary?
10. Tell briefly what each of the following signifies: Myopia, efferent nerves, paralysis, insomnia, mucus membrane.

End Notes

Chapter One

[1] This family story was verified in an article written by Rev. James M. Replogle which was published in *The Evangel*, Vol. XL, No.1 (January 1921):7.

[2] Dills, R.S. *History of Green County, Together with Historical Notes on the Northwest, and the State of Ohio.* (Dayton: Odell & Mayer, 1881): 576.

[3] Clay, Xanthe. "Return of the Mild Bunch." *The Telegraph*, November 8, 2014. Accessed July 6, 2015. http://www.telegraph.co.uk/foodanddrink/11216794/Return-of-the-mild-bunch.html.

[4] Church, Joanna. *Melodeon, 1850s-1900s.* https://afinecollection.wordpress.com/2014/07/16/melodeon-1850s-1900s/.

[5] Siebert, Wilbur Henry. *The Government of Ohio, Its History and Administration*, By Wilbur H. Siebert. (New York: Macmillan Co, 1904):157.

[6] Williams, Henry Graham. *Boxwell-Patterson Examinations: Being a Complete List of All Questions Issued by the State Commissioner of Schools Since the Patterson Law Went Into Effect. Comp. for the Use of Teachers Who Are Preparing Pupils for the Patterson Examinations Or for Admission to High School, And for Pupils for Home Study.* Athens, O.: The Ohio Teacher, 1912.

Chapter Two

[7] *Memoirs: David C. Cook, the Friend of the Sunday School.* Elgin, IL: David C. Cook Publishing Company, 1929.

[8] Columbus Avenue United Brethren Church (Springfield, Ohio), Young People's Society of Christian Endeavor. March 6, 1904. "Resolution of Respect and Condolences Upon the Death of Lottie Hoyle." Manuscript in author's personal possession.

[9] International Sunday-School Convention of the United States and British American Provinces. *The Development of the Sunday-School, 1780-1905. The Official Report of the Eleventh International Sunday-School Convention, Toronto, Canada, June 23-27, 1905.* (1905): 465-471. and

International Sunday-school Convention of the United States and British American Provinces. *Organized Sunday-School Work in America, 1905-1908; Triennial Survey of Sunday-School Work Including the Official Report of the Twelfth International Sunday School Convention, Louisville, Kentucky, June 18-23, 1908, Sunday-School Statistics Revised to Date.* (Chicago: Executive committee of the International Sunday-school Association, 1908): p 656.

[10] International Sunday-School Convention of the United States and British American Provinces. *The Development of the Sunday-School, 1780-1905: The Official Report of the Eleventh International Sunday-School Convention, Toronto, Canada, June 23-27, 1905.* Boston, Mass: Executive Committee of the International Sunday-school Association, 1971, p 467.

[11] Ibid.

[12] See for example: Behney, J. Bruce, Paul Himmel Eller, and Kenneth W. Krueger. *The History of the Evangelical United Brethren Church.* Nashville: Abingdon, 1979 and Owen, John Wilson. *A Short History of the United Brethren Church.* Dayton, OH: General Board of Christian Education, United Brethren in Christ, 1944.

[13] United Brethren General Conference. *Official Report, 1909.* Dayton, Ohio: United Brethren Pub. House, 1909.

Chapter Three

[14] "History of the United Theological Seminary." Accessed November 12, 2015. http://united.edu/history/.

[15] "Women as Clergy." Ontario Consultants on Religious Tolerance. December 30, 2015. Accessed February 3, 2016. http://www.religioustolerance.org/femclrg13.htm and Masci, David. "The Divide Over Ordaining Women." Pew Research Center. *The Pew Research Center Numbers, Facts and Trends Shaping Your World.* Washington, DC: The Pew Research Center, 1990. Accessed October 10, 2015. http://pewresearch.org/, September 9, 2014.

[16] *Seminary Bulletin: Catalogue and Alumni Number*, Vol II, No. 5, April 1906. (Dayton: Union Biblical Seminary): 5.

[17] *Seminary Bulletin: Catalogue and Alumni Number*, Vol III, No. 10, April 1907. (Dayton: Union Biblical Seminary): 20–21.

END NOTES | 197

[18] *Seminary Bulletin: Catalogue and Alumni Number*, Vol II, No. 5, April 1906. (Dayton: Union Biblical Seminary):14–15.
[19] Bonebrake Theological Seminary (Dayton, Ohio). *Souvenir: Fortieth Anniversary of the Bonebrake Theological Seminary, Formerly Union Biblical Seminary, May 2, 1912.* 1912.
[20] Hoyle, Maud E. "An Improvement on Yankee Doodle." Manuscript in author's personal possession.
[21] Hoyle, Maud E. *Thesis: Practical Christianity*. Manuscript in author's personal possession.
[22] Church of the United Brethren in Christ (New constitution). *Origin, Doctrine, Constitution, and Discipline of the United Brethren in Christ.* (Dayton, O.: United Brethren Publishing house, 1905): 44–46.
[23] Church of the United Brethren in Christ (New Constitution). *Minutes of the One Hundredth Annual Session, Miami Conference, Church of the United Brethren in Christ.* (Ohio: The Conference, 1909): 74–75.

Chapter Four

[24] Hoyle, Maud E. *Salvation.* Sermon given at Lagonda United Brethren Church, Springfield, Ohio, February 20, 1910. Unpublished manuscript in author's personal possession.
[25] Hoyle, Maud E. *Columbus Avenue E. U. B. Church.* Unpublished manuscript.
[26] Gabriel, Charles H and Johnson Oatman. *Plant My Feet on Solid Ground.* (1898).
[27] Furstenberger, A. J. "Historical Sketch." *Church Record for Columbus Ave. Society of the Church of the United Brethren in Christ at Springfield, Ohio.* (1935) Unpublished. Archives of the Brighton United Methodist Church, South Vienna, Ohio.
[28] Church of the United Brethren in Christ (New Constitution). *Minutes of the One Hundred and Fourth Annual Session, Miami Conference, Church of the United Brethren in Christ.* (Ohio: The Conference, 1913): 48.
[29] Behney, J. Bruce, Paul Himmel Eller, and Kenneth W. Krueger. *The History of the Evangelical United Brethren Church.* Nashville: Abingdon, 1979: 117.

30 Church of the United Brethren in Christ (New constitution). *Origin, Doctrine, Constitution, and Discipline of the United Brethren in Christ.* (Dayton, O.: United Brethren Publishing house, 1909): 63.

Chapter Five
31 Committee for the Study of Nursing Education / Goldmark, Josephine. *Nursing and Nursing Education in the United States.* (New York: The Macmillan Company, 1923):188.
32 "History of Community Mercy Health Partners." Accessed April 30, 2016. http://www.community-mercy.org/history2.asp
33 Prince, Benjamin F. *A Standard History of Springfield and Clark County, Ohio; An Authentic Narrative of the Past, with Particular Attention to the Modern Era in the Commercial, Industrial, Educational, Civic and Social Development.* (Chicago and New York: American Historical Society, 1922): 425–431.
34 Committee for the Study of Nursing Education / Goldmark, Josephine. *Nursing and Nursing Education in the United States.* New York: The Macmillan Company, 1923, and National League of Nursing Education. *Standard Curriculum for Schools of Nursing.* New York: National League of Nursing, 1919.
35 Committee for the Study of Nursing Education / Goldmark, Josephine. *Nursing and Nursing Education in the United States.* (New York: The Macmillan Company, 1923):348–349.

Chapter Six
36 Church of the United Brethren in Christ (New constitution). *Manual of the Woman's Missionary Association of the United Brethren in Christ for the Use of Missionaries and Missionary Candidates.* Dayton, Ohio: Woman's Missionary Association, 1894 and United Brethren in Christ. *The Missionary Manual.* Dayton, Ohio: Foreign Missionary Society, United Brethren in Christ, 1924.
37 Church of the United Brethren in Christ (New constitution). *Manual of the Woman's Missionary Association of the United Brethren in Christ for the Use of Missionaries and Missionary Candidates.* (Dayton, Ohio: Woman's Missionary Association, 1894): 26–28.
38 United Brethren in Christ. *The Missionary Manual.* (Dayton,

Ohio: Foreign Missionary Society, United Brethren in Christ, 1924):10.

[39] Church of the United Brethren in Christ (New constitution). *Manual of the Woman's Missionary Association of the United Brethren in Christ for the Use of Missionaries and Missionary Candidates.* (Dayton, Ohio: Woman's Missionary Association, 1894): 9–10.

[40] The following sources were used to write this section: Alie, Joe A. D. *A New History of Sierra Leone.* New York: St. Martin's Press, 1990; Fyfe, Christopher. *A History of Sierra Leone.* [London]: Oxford University Press, 1962; Goddard, Thomas Nelson. *The Handbook of Sierra Leone.* London: G. Richards Ltd, 1925; Kaplan, Irving. *Area Handbook for Sierra Leone.* Washington: For sale by the Supt. of Docs., U.S. Govt. Print. Off, 1976.; Karefa-Smart, John Albert Musselman. *Rainbow Happenings: A Memoir.* [United States?]: Xlibris, 2010; Karefa-Smart, John, and Rena Karefa-Smart. *The Halting Kingdom: Christianity and the African Revolution.* New York: Friendship Press, 1959; "Sierra Leone." *Wikipedia: The Free Encyclopedia.* Wikimedia Foundation Inc. Updated 4 June 2016. Encyclopedia on-line. Available from Encyclopedia on-line. Available from https://en.wikipedia.org/wiki/Sierra_Leone. Internet. Retrieved 6 June 2016.

[41] Fyfe, Christopher. *A History of Sierra Leone.* [London]: Oxford University Press, 1962:1.

[42] *African Continent* by derivative work: Bobarino (talk) African_continent-fr.svg: Eric Gaba (Sting - fr:Sting) (African_continent-fr.svg) [CC BY-SA 2.5-2.0-1.0 (http://creativecommons.org/licenses/by-sa/2.5-2.0-1.0)], via Wikimedia Commons.

[43] "Bumpeh Chiefdom, Sierra Leone." *It's All About Culture.* Accessed July 10, 2016. http://itsallaboutculture.com/bumpeh-chiefdom-sierra-leone-west-africa/.

[44] Letter from Lloyd Mignerey to Friends, July 31, 1922, *Mignerey Collection*, Otterbein University Archives.

[45] The following sources were used to write this section: Church of the United Brethren in Christ (1800-1889). *History of the Woman's Missionary Association of the United Brethren in Christ.* Dayton,

Ohio: United Brethren Pub. House, 1910; Evangelical United Brethren Church. *Proclaiming the Gospel in Africa: Sierra Leone [and] Nigeria*. Dayton, Ohio: Dept. of World Missions, Evangelical United Brethren Church, 1952; Gess, Lowell. "The Evangelical United Brethren Church in Sierra Leone." *Telescope-Messenger: Center for the EUB Heritage*. Vol 12, No. 1 (Winter 2002); Harford, Lillian Resler, and Alice Estella Bell. *History of the Women's Missionary Association of the United Brethren in Christ*. Dayton, Ohio: [United Brethren Pub. House], 1921; Hough, S. S. *Faith That Achieved: A History of the Women's Missionary Association of the Church of the United Brethren in Christ, 1872-1946*. 1958.

[46] Gess, Lowell. "The Evangelical United Brethren Church in Sierra Leone." *Telescope-Messenger: Center for the EUB Heritage*. Vol 12, No. 1 (Winter 2002):3

[47] Behney, J. Bruce, Paul Himmel Eller, and Kenneth W. Krueger. *The History of the Evangelical United Brethren Church*. (Nashville: Abingdon, 1979): 261.

[48] Ibid.

[49] Robert, Dana Lee. *American Women in Mission: A Social History of Their Thought and Practice*. (Macon, Ga: Mercer University Press, 1996): 267.

[50] Karefa-Smart, John Albert Musselman. *Rainbow Happenings: A Memoir*. ([United States?]: Xlibris, 2010):21.

[51] Hoerner, L. May. "Domestic Sciences Versus Unscientific Domesticity." *The Evangel*. Vol. XL, No. 5 (May 1921);138–141 and Wilson, Naomi R. "In the Lillian R. Harford School for Girls." *The Evangel*. XLVIII. No.1 (January1929): 7–10.

[52] Schutz, Walter. *Diary and Notes for June 2, 1923–April 5, 1951*.

[53] Robert, Dana Lee. *American Women in Mission: A Social History of Their Thought and Practice*. (Macon, Ga: Mercer University Press, 1996):414.

[54] Karefa-Smart, John, and Rena Karefa-Smart. *The Halting Kingdom: Christianity and the African Revolution*. (New York: Friendship Press, 1959):33.

[55] Ibid., 19.

[56] Letter to Rev. and Mrs. Lester Leach, dated March 14, 1929, *Board of Missions, Sierra Leone, 1911–1948*.

[57] Church of the United Brethren in Christ (New constitution). *Manual of the Woman's Missionary Association of the United*

Brethren in Christ for the Use of Missionaries and Missionary Candidates. (Dayton, Ohio: Woman's Missionary Association, 1894):29.

[58] Letter to Rev. E. M. Hursh in Freetown, Sierra Leone, dated October 16, 1920, *Board of Missions, Sierra Leone, 1911–1948.*

[59] Replogle, Rev. James. M "Miss Maud E. Hoyle." *The Evangel.* Vol. XL, No. 1 (January 1921): 7.

[60] Hoyle, Maud E. "Commissioned for His Service." *The Evangel.* Vol. XL, No. 1 (January 1921):8.

[61] United Brethren in Christ. *The Missionary Manual.* (Dayton, Ohio: Foreign Missionary Society, United Brethren in Christ, 1924):25–26.

[62] Letter from Lloyd Mignerey letter to parents, January 26, 1922, *Board of Missions, Sierra Leone, 1911–1948.*

[63] Passenger Lists leaving UK 1890–1960. *Find My Past.* Online. http://www.findmypast.co.uk/

[64] Letter from Lloyd Mignerey letter to parents, dated January 26, 1922, *Board of Missions, Sierra Leone, 1911–1948.*

Chapter Seven

[65] Letter from Lloyd Mignerey to Friends, May 20, 1922, *Mignerey Collection*, Otterbein University Archives.

[66] Information about the mission house and life on the mission was drawn from Mignerey's letters dated March 14, 1922 and August 16, 1922, *Mignerey Collection*, Otterbein University Archives; Karefa-Smart, John Albert Musselman. *Rainbow Happenings: A Memoir.* ([United States?]: Xlibris, 2010), Schutz, Walter. *Diary and Notes* for June 2, 1923–April 5, 1951.

[67] Vesper, Nora. "Hatfield–Archer Dispensary." *The Evangel.* Vol XLIII, No 3 (March 1924): 73–74.

[68] Letter from Lloyd Mignerey to Friends, September 27, 1922, *Mignerey Collection*, Otterbein University Archives.

[69] Vesper, Nora. "Hatfield-Archer Dispensary." *The Evangel.* Vol XLIII, No 3 (March 1924): 74.

[70] Letter from Lloyd Mignerey to Friends, May 22, 1922, *Mignerey Collection*, Otterbein University Archives.

[71] Letter from Lloyd Mignerey to Mrs. S. W. Kiester, June 10, 1922, *Mignerey Collection*, Otterbein University Archives.

[72] Letter from Ruth Mignerey to Mary Irene, February 22, 1922,

Mignerey Collection, Otterbein University Archives.

[73] Smith, Jeremy H. *The Staircase of a Patron: Sierra Leone and the United Brethren in Christ*. Lexington, KY: Emeth Press, 2011: 69.

[74] Schutz, Walter. "Sharing in the Evangelization of Africa". *The Evangel*. Vol. XLIII, No. 9 (September 1924): 250–252.

[75] Smith, Jeremy H. *The Staircase of a Patron: Sierra Leone and the United Brethren in Christ*. (Lexington, KY: Emeth Press, 2011): 93–95.

[76] Bachman, Susan C. "'Gospeling' in Sierra Leone" *The Evangel*. Vol. XLVII, No. 12 (December 1928): 338–341.

[77] Evangelical United Brethren Church. *Report of the Twelfth Annual Meeting, Board of Missions, the Evangelical United Brethren Church, September 24-26, 1958*: 48–49. <http://archive.org/details/reportoftwelftha00evan>.

[78] Letter from Maud Hoyle to Mrs. Mignerey, August 9, 1922. *Mignerey Collection*, Otterbein University Archives.

[79] Mignerey, Rev. L. B. "Moyamba Commencement Exercises." *The Evangel*. Vol. XLII, No. 28 (July–August 1923): 205–206.

[80] Hoyle, Maud. 1923 Annual Report. *Board of Missions, Sierra Leone, 1911–1948*.

[81] Ibid.

[82] Ibid

[83] Church of the United Brethren in Christ (New constitution). *Manual of the Woman's Missionary Association of the United Brethren in Christ for the Use of Missionaries and Missionary Candidates*. (Dayton, Ohio: Woman's Missionary Association, 1894):14.

[84] United Brethren in Christ. *The Missionary Manual*. Dayton, Ohio: Foreign Missionary Society, United Brethren in Christ, 1924: 16–17.

[85] Ancestry.com. *New York, Passenger Lists, 1820–1957* [database on-line]. Provo, UT, USA: Ancestry.com Operations, Inc., 2010.

[86] Hoyle, Maud E. "Facing Toward Africa Again." *The Evangel*. Vol. XLIII, No. 6 (June 1924):169.

[87] *Daily Times* (New Philadelphia, Ohio), March 12, 1924: 3.

[88] Hoyle, Maud E. "Facing Toward Africa Again." *The Evangel*. Vol. XLIII, No. 6 (June 1924):169.

[89] Hoyle, Maud. "Medical Work – the Need and How It is Being Met"

The Evangel. Vol. XLIV, No. 10 (October 1925): 285–286.

[90] Ancestry.com. *New York, Passenger Lists, 1820-1957* [database on-line]. Provo, UT, USA: Ancestry.com Operations, Inc., 2010.

[91] "W.M.A. Notes." *Miami Messenger*, Vol II, No. 3(November 1926): 8.

[92] "Hyde Park" *Cincinnati Enquirer*, Nov. 28, 1926: 97.

[93] General Secretary, United Brethren Board of Missions. Letter to Maud Hoyle. May 24, 1927. *Board of Missions, Sierra Leone, 1911-1948*.

[94] Hoyle, Maud. Letter to "Evangel Readers." *The Evangel.* Vol. XLVI, No. 5 (May 1927):157.

[95] Hoyle, M. E. "Council Report 1928." *Board of Missions, Sierra Leone, 1911-1948*.

[96] Ibid.

[97] Hoyle, M. E. "Personal Report for the year 1929." *Board of Missions, Sierra Leone, 1911-1948*.

[98] Leader, Charles W. "Letter to Rev. Ziegler." July 1, 1929. *Board of Missions, Sierra Leone, 1911-1948*.

[99] Hoyle, Maude. "Medical Work in Rotifunk, Taiama, and Jiama, Sierra Leone, West Africa." *The Evangel.* Vol XLIX, No. 12 (December 1930): 336.

[100] Robert, Dana Lee. *American Women in Mission: A Social History of Their Thought and Practice.* (Macon, Ga: Mercer University Press, 1996): xvii-xviii.

[101] Williams, T. B. "Miss Maud E. Hoyle." *The Evangel.* Vol XLIX, No. 10 (October 1930): 279.

Chapter Eight

[102] Ancestry.com. *New York, Passenger Lists, 1820-1957* [database on-line]. Provo, UT, USA: Ancestry.com Operations, Inc., 2010.

[103] *The Pantagraph* (Bloomington, Illinois), October 12, 1930: 11.

[104] Evangelical United Brethren Church. *Report of the Twelfth Annual Meeting, Board of Missions, the Evangelical United Brethren Church, September 24-26, 1958*: 47–48.

[105] *The Richmond Item* (Richmond, Indiana), October 7, 1931: 2.

[106] *Palladium Item* (Richmond, Indiana), September 18, 1931: 9.

[107] Evangelical United Brethren Church. *Report of the Twelfth Annual Meeting, Board of Missions, the Evangelical United Brethren*

Church, September 24-26, 1958.: 47–48. 1958. <http://archive.org/details/reportoftwelftha00evan>.

[108] Ancestry.com. *1940 United States Federal Census* [database online]. Provo, UT, USA: Ancestry.com Operations, Inc., 2012.

[109] Tennant, Anna Marie. "From the Window." *Springfield News & Sun*, n.d.

[110] Church of the United Brethren in Christ (New constitution), John Wilson Owen, and W. E. Snyder. *Discipline of the Church of the United Brethren in Christ: Including Origin, Doctrine, and Constitution, 1941-1945*. Dayton, Ohio: Otterbein Press, 1941.

[111] Peckham, Arline B. *Faces of the Spirit: A History of Otterbein Home 1912-1987*. [Place of publication not identified]: [publisher not identified], 1987: 25.

[112] Risley, Mrs. F. A. "Matron's Report." *The Otterbein Home News*, April–June 1955: 12.

[113] Evangelical United Brethren Church. *Minutes of the ... Session of the Ohio Miami Conference ... of the Evangelical United Brethren Church*. 1952: 92–93.

[114] Ibid.

Bibliography

African Continent by derivative work: Bobarino (talk) African_continent-fr.svg: Eric Gaba (Sting - fr:Sting) (African_continent-fr.svg) [CC BY-SA 2.5-2.0-1.0 (http://creativecommons.org/licenses/by-sa/2.5-2.0-1.0)], via Wikimedia Commons.

Alie, Joe A. D. *A New History of Sierra Leone.* New York: St. Martin's Press, 1990.

Ancestry.com. *1940 United States Federal Census* [database on-line]. Provo, UT, USA: Ancestry.com Operations, Inc., 2012.

Ancestry.com. *New York, Passenger Lists, 1820-1957* [database on-line]. Provo, UT, USA: Ancestry.com Operations, Inc., 2010.

Bachman, Susan C. "'Gospeling' in Sierra Leone." *The Evangel.* Vol. XLVII, No. 12 (December 1928): 338–341.

Behney, J. Bruce, Paul Himmel Eller, and Kenneth W. Krueger. *The History of the Evangelical United Brethren Church.* Nashville: Abingdon, 1979.

Bonebrake Theological Seminary (Dayton, Ohio). *Souvenir: Fortieth Anniversary of the Bonebrake Theological Seminary, Formerly Union Biblical Seminary, May 2, 1912.* 1912.

"Bumpeh Chiefdom, Sierra Leone." *It's All About Culture.* Accessed July 10, 1016. http://itsallaboutculture.com/bumpeh-chiefdom-sierra-leone-west-africa/.

Church, Joanna. *Melodeon, 1850s-1900s.* https://afinecollection.wordpress.com/ 2014/07/ 16/melodeon-1850s-1900s/.

Church of the United Brethren in Christ (1800-1889). *History of the Woman's Missionary Association of the United Brethren in Christ.* Dayton, Ohio: United Brethren Pub. House, 1910.

Church of the United Brethren in Christ (1800-1889). Evangelical United Brethren Church. *Proclaiming the Gospel in Africa: Sierra Leone [and] Nigeria.* Dayton, Ohio: Dept. of World Missions, Evangelical United Brethren Church, 1952.

Church of the United Brethren in Christ (New constitution), John Wilson Owen, and W. E. Snyder. *Discipline of the Church of the United Brethren in Christ: Including Origin, Doctrine, and*

Constitution, 1941-1945; [Edited by J.W. Owen and W.E. Snyder]. Dayton, Ohio: Otterbein Press, 1941.

Church of the United Brethren in Christ (New constitution). *The Evangel.* Dayton, Ohio: Women's Missionary Association of the United Brethren in Christ, 1918-1946.

Church of the United Brethren in Christ (New constitution). *Manual of the Woman's Missionary Association of the United Brethren in Christ for the Use of Missionaries and Missionary Candidates.* Dayton, Ohio: Woman's Missionary Association, 1894.

Church of the United Brethren in Christ (New Constitution). *Minutes of the One Hundredth Annual Session, Miami Conference, Church of the United Brethren in Christ.* Ohio: The Conference, 1909.

Church of the United Brethren in Christ (New Constitution). *Minutes of the One Hundred and Fourth Annual Session, Miami Conference, Church of the United Brethren in Christ.* Ohio: The Conference, 1913.

Church of the United Brethren in Christ (New constitution). *Origin, Doctrine, Constitution, and Discipline of the United Brethren in Christ.* Dayton, O.: United Brethren Publishing house, 1905.

Church of the United Brethren in Christ (New constitution). *Origin, Doctrine, Constitution, and Discipline of the United Brethren in Christ.* Dayton, O.: United Brethren Publishing house, 1909.

Clay, Xanthe. "Return of the Mild Bunch." *The Telegraph*, November 8, 2014. Accessed February 2, 2016. http://www.telegraph.co.uk/foodanddrink/11216794/Return-of-the-mild-bunch.html.

Columbus Avenue United Brethren Church (Springfield, Ohio), Young People's Society of Christian Endeavor. March 6, 1904. "Resolution of Respect and Condolences Upon the Death of Lottie Hoyle." Manuscript in author's personal possession.

Committee for the Study of Nursing Education / Goldmark, Josephine. *Nursing and Nursing Education in the United States.* New York: The Macmillan Company, 1923.

Daily Times (New Philadelphia, Ohio), March 12, 1924: 3.

Dills, R.S. *History of Green County, Together with Historical Notes on the Northwest, and the State of Ohio.* Dayton: Odell & Mayer, 1881.

Evangelical United Brethren Church. *Minutes of the ... Session of the Ohio Miami Conference ... of the Evangelical United Brethren Church.* 1952: 92–93.

Evangelical United Brethren Church. *Proclaiming the Gospel in Africa: Sierra Leone [and] Nigeria.* Dayton, Ohio: Dept. of World Missions, Evangelical United Brethren Church, 1952.

Evangelical United Brethren Church. *Report of the Twelfth Annual Meeting, Board of Missions, the Evangelical United Brethren Church, September 24-26, 1958*: 47–49. <http://archive.org/details/reportoftwelftha00evan>.

Fluehr-Lobban, Carolyn, Lobban, Richard, Zangari, Linda. "'Tribe': A Socio-Political Analysis." *Ufahamu: a Journal of African Studies.* Vol.7, No.1 (1976): 143–165. <http://escholarship.org/uc/item/6fs3g8wh#page-2>

Frisbie, Julia. "Rotifunk Hospital Re-Opens." United Methodist Committee on Relief. News Archives. June 19, 2014. http://www.umcor.org/UMCOR/Resources/News-Stories/2014/June/0619rotifunk.)

Furstenberger, A. J. "Historical Sketch." *Church Record for Columbus Ave. Society of the Church of the United Brethren in Christ at Springfield, Ohio.* (1935) Unpublished. Archives of the Brighton United Methodist Church, South Vienna, Ohio.

Fyfe, Christopher. *A History of Sierra Leone.* [London]: Oxford University Press, 1962.

Gabriel, Charles H. and Johnson Oatman. *Plant My Feet on Solid Ground* (1898).

General Secretary, United Brethren Board of Missions. Letter to Maud Hoyle. May 24, 1927. *Board of Missions, Sierra Leone, 1911-1948.*

Gess, Lowell. "The Evangelical United Brethren Church in Sierra Leone." *Telescope-Messenger: Center for the EUB Heritage.* Vol 12, No. 1(Winter 2002): 2–4.

Goddard, Thomas Nelson. *The Handbook of Sierra Leone.* London: G. Richards Ltd, 1925.

Harford, Lillian Resler, and Alice Estella Bell. *History of the Women's Missionary Association of the United Brethren in Christ.* Dayton, Ohio: [United Brethren Pub. House], 1921.

"History of Community Mercy Health Partners." Accessed April 30, 2016. http://www.community-mercy.org/history2.asp.

"History of the United Theological Seminary." Accessed March 5, 2016. http://united.edu/history/.

Hoerner, L. May. "Domestic Sciences Versus Unscientific Domesticity." *The Evangel.* Vol. XL, No. 5 (May 1921):138–141.

Hough, S. S. *Faith That Achieved: A History of the Women's Missionary Association of the Church of the United Brethren in Christ, 1872-1946.* 1958.

Hoyle, M. E. "Council Report 1928." *Board of Missions, Sierra Leone, 1911-1948.*

Hoyle, M. E. "Personal Report for the year 1929." *Board of Missions, Sierra Leone, 1911-1948.*

Hoyle, Maud E. "1923 Annual Report." *Board of Missions, Sierra Leone, 1911-1948.*

Hoyle, Maud E. *Columbus Avenue E. U. B. Church.* Unpublished manuscript in author's personal possession.

Hoyle, Maud E. "Commissioned for His Service." *The Evangel.* Vol. XL, No. 1 (January 1921):8.

Hoyle, Maud E. "Facing Toward Africa Again." *The Evangel.* Vol. XLIII, No. 6 (June 1924):169.

Hoyle, Maud E. "An Improvement on Yankee Doodle." Manuscript in author's personal possession.

Hoyle, Maud. Letter to "Evangel Readers." *The Evangel.* Vol. XLVI, No. 5 (May 1927):157.

Hoyle, Maud E. Letter to "Mrs. Mignerey." August 9, 1922. *Mignerey Collection*, Otterbein University Archives.

Hoyle, Maude. "Medical Work in Rotifunk, Taiama, and Jiama, Sierra Leone, West Africa." *The Evangel.* Vol XLIX, No. 12 (December 1930): 336.

Hoyle, Maud. "Medical Work – the Need and How It is Being Met" *The Evangel.* Vol. XLIV, No. 10 (October 1925): 285–286.

Hoyle, Maud E. *Salvation.* Sermon given at Lagonda United Brethren Church, Springfield, Ohio, February 20, 1910. Unpublished manuscript in author's personal possession.

Hoyle, Maud E. *Thesis: Practical Christianity.* Manuscript in author's personal possession.

"Hyde Park" *Cincinnati Enquirer*, Nov. 28, 1926: 97.

International Sunday-School Convention of the United States and British American Provinces. *The Development of the Sunday-School, 1780-1905. The Official Report of the Eleventh*

International Sunday-School Convention, Toronto, Canada, June 23-27, 1905. 1905.

International Sunday-school Convention of the United States and British American Provinces. *Organized Sunday-School Work in America, 1905-1908; Triennial Survey of Sunday-School Work Including the Official Report of the Twelfth International Sunday School Convention, Louisville, Kentucky, June 18-23, 1908, Sunday-School Statistics Revised to Date*. Chicago: Executive Committee of the International Sunday-School Association, 1908.

Kachel, Charles E. "Similarities and Differences Between the Methodist Church and the Evangelical United Brethren Church." *Methodist History*. (October 1964):12–22.

Kaplan, Irving. *Area Handbook for Sierra Leone*. Washington: For sale by the Supt. of Docs., U.S. Govt. Print. Off, 1976.

Karefa-Smart, John Albert Musselman. *Rainbow Happenings: A Memoir*. [United States?]: Xlibris, 2010.

Karefa-Smart, John, and Rena Karefa-Smart. *The Halting Kingdom: Christianity and the African Revolution*. New York: Friendship Press, 1959.

Leader, Charles W. "Letter to Rev. Ziegler." July 1, 1929. *Board of Missions, Sierra Leone, 1911-1948*.

Letter to Rev. and Mrs. Lester Leach, dated March 14, 1929, *Board of Missions, Sierra Leone, 1911-1948*.

Letter to Rev. E. M. Hursh in Freetown, Sierra Leone, dated October 16, 1920, *Board of Missions, Sierra Leone, 1911-1948*.

McElfresh, Franklin. *The Training of Sunday School Teachers and Officers*. New York: Eaton & Mains, 1914.

Masci, David. "The Divide Over Ordaining Women." Pew Research Center. *The Pew Research Center Numbers, Facts and Trends Shaping Your World*. Washington, DC: The Pew Research Center, 1990. <http://pewresearch.org/>, September 9, 2014.

Memoirs: David C. Cook, the Friend of the Sunday School. Elgin, IL: David C. Cook Publishing Company, 1929.

Mignerey Collection, Otterbein University Archives.

Mignerey, Lloyd. Letter to "Friends." May 20, 1922, *Mignerey Collection*, Otterbein University Archives.

Mignerey, Lloyd. Letter to "Friends." May 22, 1922, *Mignerey Collection*, Otterbein University Archives.

Mignerey, Lloyd. Letter to "Friends." July 31, 1922, *Mignerey Collection*, Otterbein University Archives.

Mignerey, Lloyd. Letter to "Friends." September 27, 1922, *Mignerey Collection*, Otterbein University Archives.

Mignerey, Lloyd. Letter to "Mrs. S. W. Kiester, June 10, 1922, Mignerey Collection, Otterbein University Archives.

Mignerey, Lloyd. Letter to "Parents." January 26, 1922, *Board of Missions, Sierra Leone, 1911-1948*.

Mignerey, Rev. L. B. "Moyamba Commencement Exercises." *The Evangel*. Vol. XLII, No. 28 (July–August 1923): 205–206.

Mignerey, Ruth. Letter to "Mary Irene." February 22, 1922, *Mignerey Collection*, Otterbein University Archives.

National League of Nursing Education. *Standard Curriculum for Schools of Nursing*. New York: National League of Nursing, 1919.

Outten, Bridgette. "Church Has Last Service." *Springfield News-Sun*. December 27, 2009.

Owen, John Wilson. *A Short History of the United Brethren Church*. Dayton, OH: General Board of Christian Education, United Brethren in Christ, 1944.

Palladium Item (Richmond, Indiana), September 18, 1931: 9.

The Pantagraph (Bloomington, Illinois), October 12, 1930: 11.

Passenger Lists leaving UK 1890-1960. *Find My Past*. Online. http://www.findmypast.co.uk/.

Peckham, Arline B. *Faces of the Spirit: A History of Otterbein Home 1912-1987*. [Place of publication not identified]: [publisher not identified], 1987: 25.

Prince, Benjamin F. *A Standard History of Springfield and Clark County, Ohio; An Authentic Narrative of the Past, with Particular Attention to the Modern Era in the Commercial, Industrial, Educational, Civic and Social Development*. Chicago and New York: American Historical Society, 1922.

Replogle, Rev. James. M "Miss Maud E. Hoyle." *The Evangel*. Vol. XL, No. 1 (January 1921): 7.

The Richmond Item (Richmond, Indiana), October 7, 1931: 2.

Risley, Mrs. F. A. "Matron's Report." *The Otterbein Home News*, April-June 1955: 12.

Robert, Dana Lee. *American Women in Mission: A Social History of Their Thought and Practice*. Macon, Ga: Mercer University Press, 1996.

Schutz, Walter. *Diary and Notes for June 2, 1923 - April 5, 1951.* 1923.

Schutz, Walter. "Sharing in the Evangelization of Africa". *The Evangel.* Vol. XLIII, No. 9 (September 1924): 250–252.

Seminary Bulletin: *Catalogue and Alumni Number*, Vol II, No. 5, April 1906. Dayton: Union Biblical Seminary.

Seminary Bulletin: *Catalogue and Alumni Number*, Vol III, No. 10, April 1907. Dayton: Union Biblical Seminary.

Siebert, Wilbur Henry. *The Government of Ohio, Its History and Administration.* New York: Macmillan Co, 1904.

"Sierra Leone." *Wikipedia: The Free Encyclopedia.* Wikimedia Foundation Inc. Updated 4 June 2016. Encyclopedia on-line. Available from Encyclopedia on-line. Available from https://en.wikipedia.org/wiki/Sierra_Leone. Internet. Retrieved 6 June 2016.

Smith, Jeremy H. *The Staircase of a Patron: Sierra Leone and the United Brethren in Christ.* Lexington, KY: Emeth Press, 2011.

Tennant, Anna Marie. "From the Window." *Springfield News & Sun,* n.d.

Trager, James. *The People's Chronology: A Year-by-Year Record of Human Events from Prehistory to the Present.* New York: H. Holt, 1992.

United Brethren General Conference. *Official Report, 1909.* Dayton, Ohio: United Brethren Pub. House, 1909.

United Brethren in Christ. *The Church Annual; Yearbook of the United Brethren in Christ,* 1946.

United Brethren in Christ. *The Missionary Manual.* Dayton, Ohio: Foreign Missionary Society, United Brethren in Christ, 1924.

United Methodist Church (U.S.), Church of the United Brethren in Christ (New constitution), and Scholarly Resources Inc. *Board of Missions, Sierra Leone, 1911-1948,* 1998.

Vesper, Nora. "Hatfield-Archer Dispensary." *The Evangel.* Vol XLIII, No 3 (March 1924): 73–74.

Williams, Henry Graham. *Boxwell-Patterson Examinations: Being a Complete List of All Questions Issued by the State Commissioner of Schools Since the Patterson Law Went Into Effect. Comp. for the Use of Teachers Who Are Preparing Pupils for the Patterson Examinations Or for Admission to High School, And for Pupils for Home Study.* Athens, O.: The Ohio Teacher, 1912.

Williams, T. B. "Miss Maud E. Hoyle." *The Evangel.* Vol XLIX, No. 10 (October 1930): 279.

Wilson, Naomi R. "In the Lillian R. Harford School for Girls." *The Evangel.* XLVIII. No.1 (January 1929): 7–10.

"W.M.A. Notes." *Miami Messenger,* Vol II, No.3 (November 1926): 8.

"Women as Clergy." Ontario Consultants on Religious Tolerance. December 30, 2015. Accessed March 10, 2016. http://www.religioustolerance.org/femclrg13.htm

Made in the USA
Middletown, DE
14 June 2018